complete

cooking

complete
cooking

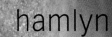

This edition first published in the U.K. in 1997 by
Hamlyn, a division of Octopus Publishing Group Limited
2–4 Heron Quays, London E14 4JP

Reprinted 2001

ISBN 0 600 60608 2

NOTES
Both metric and imperial measurements have been given in all
recipes. Use one set of measurements only, and not a mixture of
both.

Standard level spoon measurements are used in all recipes.
1 tablespoon = one 15 ml spoon
1 teaspoon = one 5 ml spoon

Eggs should be medium to large unless otherwise stated.
The Department of Health advises that eggs should not be
consumed raw. This book contains dishes made with raw or
lightly cooked eggs. It is prudent for more vulnerable people such
as pregnant and nursing mothers, invalids, the elderly, babies and
young children to avoid uncooked or lightly cooked dishes made
with eggs. Once prepared, these dishes should be kept refrigerated
and used promptly.

Meat and poultry should be cooked thoroughly. To test if poultry
is cooked, pierce the flesh through the thickest part with a skewer
or fork — the juices should run clear, never pink or red. Do not
re-freeze poultry that has been frozen previously and thawed.
Do not re-freeze a cooked dish that has been frozen previously.

Milk should be full fat unless otherwise stated.

Nut and Nut Derivatives
This book includes dishes made with nuts and nut derivatives. It
is advisable for customers with known allergic reactions to nuts
and nut derivatives and those who may be potentially vulnerable
to these allergies, such as pregnant and nursing mothers, invalids,
the elderly, babies and children to avoid dishes made with nuts
and nut oils. It is also prudent to check the labels of pre-prepared
ingredients for the possible inclusion of nut derivatives.

Pepper should be freshly ground black pepper unless otherwise
stated.

Fresh herbs should be used, unless otherwise stated. If
unavailable, use dried herbs as an alternative, but halve the
quantities stated.

Measurements for canned food have been given as a standard
metric equivalent.

Ovens should be pre-heated to the specified temperature — if
using a fan-assisted oven, follow the manufacturer's instructions
for adjusting the time and the temperature.

Vegetarians should look for the 'V' symbol on a cheese to ensure it
is made with vegetarian rennet. There are vegetarian forms of
Parmesan, feta, Cheddar, Cheshire, Red Leicester, dolcelatte and
many goats' cheeses, among others.

Contents

Introduction 6

Cook's Tools 12

Utensils 14

Soups and Starters 16

Beef, Lamb and Pork 42

Flour, Grains and Rice 56

Fish and Shellfish 72

Poultry and Game 104

Pasta and Rice 126

Oils and Vinegars 136

Vegetables 152

Vegetable Selection 168

Salads and Salad Dressings 178

Salad Leaves and Herbs 184

Desserts 202

Summer Fruit 206

Exotic Fruit 216

Baking 232

Index 252

Introduction

Mrs Beeton would be utterly amazed at the transformation that has taken place in the domestic environment since she wrote her classic book on cooking and household management. When she was writing, there were no cookers, microwaves, refrigerators, mixers, blenders or dishwashers to ease the burden of housework. In her day, it was essential that the Victorian housewife learned the skills of feeding her family in the most precise detail – from preserving fruit and vegetables to making her own cleaning materials so she could keep her kitchen fresh and clean. If she had little or no help from servants, these skills were even more important and were literally the means of her family's survival.

Today's cook faces different problems – usually because the hustle-bustle of modern life means that there is hardly a spare moment to think about what to cook for the family. There is so *much* choice, and so *many* sources of information that it can all be quite overwhelming.

If Mrs Beeton were writing now, she would have no need to go into such encyclopedic detail. Today, we can walk into our local supermarket and buy superb ingredients from every part of the globe. Also, our butchers, bakers and fishmongers will clean, fillet, dice and slice as a normal part of their service.

Essentially, the modern cook needs a generous collection of cleverly chosen, delicious recipes which exploit the brilliant resources of our food stores and supermarkets and produce varied, mouthwatering meals. Since you don't have to spend hours making your own preserves, breads and pastry (unless you want to, of course) you can turn your attention to the creative use of all those wonderful goodies that beckon temptingly from the shelves – all those glowing bottles of luscious oils, dazzling selections of wines, generous heaps of healthy fruits and vegetables, crisp salads, fresh fish and shellfish, first class meat and poultry, fragrant newly-baked bread in a tempting range of styles and flavours, intriguing spices and flavourings and fresh herbs growing in pots ready to pluck as you need them.

This is a wonderful time to be in the kitchen if you are interested in preparing delicious, adventurous food, even if you don't have a great deal of time to spend on cooking. Rather than being a slave to the kitchen sink, the modern cook can concentrate on seeking out ideas and variety. By carefully selecting dishes from all over the world, *Complete Cooking* has done the choosing for you – there are the fashionable, tangy new flavours of New World dishes, from Latin America for example, but there are also well-loved favourites, such as a delectable rose-scented rice pudding – a true English classic. *Complete Cooking* makes intelligent use of those lovely ingredients that are available from all over the world.

Storecupboard ingredients

Because our food shops offer us so much abundance, it is tempting to buy too much! There is nothing more depressing than finding that you have to throw away half-used packets of herbs, pulses and other storecupboard

It is useful to attach a label to the inside of the lid of dry goods' storage jars and make a note on it of the 'use by date' indicated on the manufacturer's packaging, especially if the ingredient is one which you use rarely. Remember to update the label when you re-stock the jar. Nowadays, many dry goods are free from preservatives and additives which prolonged their shelf life in the past. Breakfast cereals, porridge oats, sultanas, currants and other dried fruits can also be decanted into storage containers.

Fresh herbs

One way for the busy cook to achieve excellent results is to use fresh ingredients such as herbs whenever possible. These can always be judiciously combined with ready-made ingredients, and they really do make a difference to the flavour of the finished dish. If you have the chance, try growing some fresh herbs in your garden, in your window boxes, or simply buy a pot from the supermarket and keep it on the kitchen window ledge. Dried herbs are an acceptable alternative when fresh ones are not available. Buy them in small quantities, as you will only use a little at a time, and replace them regularly to avoid staleness. The herbs most commonly used in modern cooking include the following:

• Basil gives an incomparable flavour to tomato dishes. Many supermarkets now sell pots of fresh basil. Buy some – it will give your kitchen a delicious aroma.
• Parsley is excellent in virtually any savoury dish. If possible, use the flat-leaved continental variety when it is available, as it has a much better flavour.
• Coriander is delicately scented, and is an interesting alternative to parsley.
• Sage gives a rich flavour to veal and chicken dishes. It is particularly good in any dish that is cooked in wine.
• Bay leaves are used to flavour casseroles, soups and roasts and are also put on the fire at outdoor barbecues.

ingredients which have been kept well past their sell-by date, and ended up dessicated and flavourless. The best way to make use of your store cupboard is to fine-tune its contents to your preferred style of cooking. If you enjoy cooking and eating pasta on a frequent basis, but are not so fond of rice, for example, invest in a really exciting range of different varieties of pasta (in both fresh and dry form), but also keep some good quality long-grain rice in an airtight jar for basic use. Remember, packs of fresh pasta can be frozen if you don't use them on the day of purchase. Once you get used to keying your store cupboard to your culinary preferences, you'll find that there is far less waste. What you keep in your store-cupboard is entirely up to you of course – the main thing to keep in mind is that it is pointless buying masses of provisions just because you think you may get around to using them some time.

Buy your supplies in a disciplined manner to make the best use of your money and storage space. Then, if you do get an urge to experiment with an exotic new recipe, you can buy the ingredients specially.

Storecupboard supplies such as flour, rice, pulses, grain, etc. should be decanted into clean glass jars or polythene containers. These should be clearly labelled and kept airtight. There are many attractive kitchen storage jars available which are designed to keep dry goods.

- Rosemary is beautifully aromatic and has a strong flavour best suited to lamb or pork dishes. It can also be used with chicken or fish, but use it sparingly as the flavour can be too powerful.
- Oregano is used on pizzas and in casseroles and sauces.
- Thyme is available is many flavours – including lemon and apple. The classic variety has a delicious, fresh aroma, and is often included in a *bouquet garni.*
- *Bouquet garni* – this is a small bunch of herbs (usually a bay leaf and sprigs of thyme, rosemary and parsley) and sometimes a twist of orange peel. These are tied together in a small bunch and are simmered in stews and casseroles. It is removed before serving.

Specialist ingredients

As ethnic cuisines such as Indonesian, Mexican, Thai, Indian and Chinese have become increasingly popular, people want to try new dishes. Fortunately, many of the specialist ingredients required are now on sale at large supermarkets, or alternatively at ethnic food stores. When a specialist ingredient is required in one of the recipes in the book, the accompanying clipboard will provide appropriate information.

Sauces and gravies

The following sauces and gravies are used in some of the recipes in *Complete Cooking:*

Bechamel Sauce
- Put 600 ml/1 pint milk into a saucepan, and add 1 onion stuck with 2 cloves, 1 carrot cut in to quarters and a *bouquet garni.* Bring to the boil, then reduce the heat to a bare simmer. Leave the saucepan to infuse over a very low heat for 30 minutes. Melt 50 g/2 oz of butter in a clean saucepan, and stir in 50 g/2 oz of flour. Cook for 1 minute, stirring constantly to obtain a smooth roux (paste). Do not allow the roux to brown.

  Remove the pan from the heat, and gradually stir in the milk, a little at a time, stirring vigorously after each addition. The sauce should be completely smooth. Return the pan to the heat and bring slowly to the boil, stirring constantly. Lower the heat, and simmer gently for 5-6 minutes until the sauce thickens. Season with salt, freshly ground black pepper, and grated nutmeg.

Makes 600 ml/1 pint
Preparation time: *5–10 minutes*
Cooking time: *40 minutes*

Rouille (Red Pepper Sauce)
- Cut a small red pepper in half and remove the core and seeds. Chop the flesh into small pieces and crush to a paste with 2 garlic cloves in a mortar.

  Add a pinch of saffron powder and salt and freshly ground black pepper to taste. Moisten 50 g/2 oz crustless white bread with a little water (or some of the cooking liquid if making bouillabaisse).

  Work it into the pepper and garlic until thoroughly incorporated. Beat in 2 egg yolks. Add 250 ml/8 fl oz olive oil, a little at a time, beating well between each addition. As the rouille becomes thick, pour the oil in a thin, steady stream. Continue beating until the rouille is thick and smooth.

Makes 250 ml/8 fl oz
Preparation time: *15–20 minutes*

Tomato Sauce
- Put 3 tablespoons of olive oil, 1 x 425 g/14 oz can of chopped tomatoes, 1 teaspoon dried oregano, a pinch of sugar, salt and freshly ground black pepper into a saucepan, and bring to the boil. Simmer briskly, uncovered, for 20–25 minutes until the sauce is thick. Serve hot or cold as required.

Makes 425 g/14 oz
Preparation time: *2 minutes*
Cooking time: *20–25 minutes*

Salsa Cruda (Tomato Chilli Sauce)

This is a coarse-textured, uncooked sauce, used for dipping. It has a spicy flavour.
• Skin and chop 500 g/1 lb large, ripe tomatoes, deseed and finely chop 2 green chillies, and finely chop 1 onion. Put these ingredients in a bowl with a pinch of sugar, season with salt and freshly ground pepper to taste, and stir in some chopped fresh coriander.

Makes 625 g/1¼ lb
Preparation time: *10–15 minutes*

Satay Sauce

• Put 2 tablespoons of corn oil into a small pan, and add 1 large onion, finely chopped.
    Cook the onion until it is softened. Add 2 crushed garlic cloves, 2 tablespoons of crunchy peanut butter, 2 tablespoons of sweet chilli sauce, 2 teaspoons of soy sauce and 100 ml/ 3½ fl oz of boiling water. Simmer very gently for 3 minutes.
    Transfer to a serving bowl and allow to cool.
    Use this as a dipping sauce, or to coat skewers of meat ready for grilling.

Makes 175 g/6 oz
Preparation time: *5 minutes*
Cooking time: *6–8 minutes*

"... delicious, adventurous food, even if you don't have a great deal of time."

Meat Gravies

Depending on what kind of meat is being cooked, either choose a light (chicken or vegetable) or rich (beef) stock.
• Pour off all but 2 tablespoons of fat from the pan, leaving the residue. Set the meat aside while making the gravy. Add 2 tablespoons of flour to the pan, and stir over low heat until it is bubbling and golden. Gradually stir in 300 ml/½ pint of beef, chicken or vegetable stock or wine, as liked. Add salt and pepper to taste.

Makes 300 ml/½ pint
Preparation time: *2–3 minutes*
Cooking time: *4–5 minutes*

Fresh stock recipes

You will find it very useful to refer to these basic recipes as they are required throughout the book.
    A good stock is easy and cheap to make, with only a few basic ingredients. It is not necessary to resort to stock cubes, when the flavour of a fresh aromatic broth is far superior. For beef or fish stock you should be able to find the bones you need at the butcher or fishmonger.
    Once made, the stocks can be frozen when cooled. Freeze in small batches in plastic tubs or ice cube trays. When frozen, the cubes can be transferred to clearly labelled plastic bags for ease of storage.
    A few basic rules are necessary when making stock.
• Stock should always simmer extremely gently, or it will evaporate too quickly and become cloudy.
• Never add salt to the stock when cooling as simmering will reduce it and concentrate the flavour. This will affect the flavour of the finished dish.

• Any scum that rises to the surface should be removed as it will spoil the colour and flavour of the final stock.
• Avoid any floury root vegetables as these will make the stock cloudy.

Beef stock

750 g/1½lb shin of beef, cubed
2 onions, chopped
2–3 carrots, chopped
2 celery sticks, chopped
1 bay leaf
1 bouquet garni
4–6 black peppercorns
1.8 litres/3 pints water
½ teaspoon salt

• Place all the ingredients in a large saucepan. Slowly bring to the boil, and immediately reduce the heat to a slow simmer. Cover with a well-fitting lid and simmer for 4 hours, removing any scum from the surface. Strain the stock through a muslin lined sieve and leave to cool before refrigerating.

Makes about 1.5 litres/ 2½ pints
Preparation time: *15 minutes*
Cooking time: *about 4½ hours*

Chicken stock

Chicken stock is used extensively throughout the book, and a good recipe is essential to success. The following gives a light, delicately flavoured stock which has a good flavour, but will not overpower the ingredients in the final dish.

• Chop a cooked chicken carcass into 3 or 4 pieces and place it in a large saucepan with the raw giblets and trimmings, 1 roughly chopped onion, 2 roughly chopped large carrots, and 1 roughly chopped celery stalk, 1 bay leaf, a few lightly crushed parsley stalks, 1 sprig thyme and cover with 1.8 litres/3 pints cold water.
• Bring to the boil, removing any scum from the surface. Lower the heat and simmer for 2–2½ hours. Strain the stock through a muslin-lined sieve and leave to cool completely before refrigerating.

Makes 1 litre/1¾ pints
Preparation time: *5–10 minutes*
Cooking time: *about 2½ hours*

Fish stock

When purchasing the bones for this stock, avoid buying the bones of oily fish. It is very important that the stock does not boil as it will become very cloudy.
• Place 1½ kg/3 lb fish trimmings and 1 sliced onion, the white part of a small leek, 1 celery stalk, 1 bay leaf, 6 parsley stalks, 10 whole peppercorns and 475 ml/16 fl oz dry white wine into a large saucepan, and cover with 1.8 litres/3 pints cold water. Bring slowly to just below boiling point. Simmer for 20 minutes, removing any scum from the surface. Strain the stock through a muslin-lined sieve and leave to cool before refrigerating.

Makes 1.8 litres/3 pints
Preparation time: *10 minutes*
Cooking time: *20 minutes*

"... dishes from all over the world."

A note on food safety

While modern equipment like refrigerators and freezers can certainly help to keep food fresh and safe to eat, it is possible to become over-reliant on our gadgets. There is no substitute for a good routine of kitchen hygiene. This not only means that kitchen utensils and working surfaces must always be kept clean, but also that food is handled and stored correctly.

The main point to remember is that germs and bacteria thrive in warmth and moisture – so cooked food should never be left standing about in a warm room. It must be cooled rapidly, then placed in the refrigerator. You should be particularly careful of dishes like shepherd's pie, mince or meat pies, and any dishes made with milk and eggs.

Keep all cooked and pasteurized foods separate from raw foods, to avoid any contamination. Wipe any surfaces where you have been preparing raw chicken or other meat, and never place cooked food on the same surface before wiping it clean.

Unwrap raw meat or fish, put it on a plate lightly covered with greaseproof paper or clingfilm then store in the refrigerator ready for cooking. When putting the plate in the refrigerator, make sure the food does not drip on to any cooked foods on a lower shelf.

Defrost *all* meat thoroughly, especially poultry and pork. Read the instructions on the packaging for the recommended defrosting times. If the meat fails to defrost completely, it may not cook completely, and the warm, moist conditions inside the meat could cause a serious outbreak of salmonella. *Never partly cook meat or poultry ahead and then finish it later – this is very dangerous.*

Wash all fruit and salad leaves, and wipe vegetables so that they are free of any dirt. Store them carefully.

Always remember to wipe the outsides and bases of milk, juice and wine bottles before putting them in the refrigerator. Regular defrosting will ensure that your refrigerator works effectively.

Vegetable stock

This recipe makes a well-flavoured vegetable stock which makes a good basis for many recipes, and can also be varied to your own taste. Once you have made it several times, you might wish to experiment with other flavourings. You can also ring the changes according to which vegetables are in season at the time. Try adding some fennel bulb for a mild aniseed flavour, or a sliver of orange rind for an added lift. The addition of tomatoes will give it richness of flavour and colour. Avoid any floury root vegetables, however, as these will make the stock become cloudy.

• Place 500 g/1 lb chopped mixed vegetables such as carrots, leeks, celery, onion and mushrooms, using about an equal quantity of each one; 1 garlic clove ,
6 peppercorns, 1 *bouquet garni* (2 parsley sprigs, 2 thyme sprigs and 1 bay leaf) in a saucepan, and cover with 1.2 litres/2 pints water. Bring to the boil and simmer gently for 30 minutes, skimming when necessary. Strain the stock and cool it completely before refrigerating.

Makes 1 litre/1¾ pints
Preparation time: *5–10 minutes*
Cooking time: *about 45 minutes*

Cook's Tools

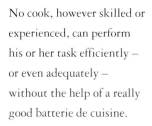

Excellence in the art of cookery, as in all other things, is only attainable by practice and experience. In proportion, therefore to the opportunities which a cook has had of these, so will be her excellence in the art.

Eliza Beeton, late 19th-century British authority on cooking and household management

No cook, however skilled or experienced, can perform his or her task efficiently – or even adequately – without the help of a really good batterie de cuisine.

Knives (chopping, paring, bread)

Perhaps above all else, a good cook needs a set of knives. These should be well maintained, cleaned and dried thoroughly, and sharpened regularly.

Chopping knife: A heavy wide-bladed knife is ideal for chopping all vegetables and other ingredients. It is also good for flattening thinly sliced meats, and transferring ingredients from the board to the pan.

Paring knife: This small knife is used for trimming and peeling vegetables.

Bread knife: A large serrated knife is good for slicing bread, cakes and pastries, as it stops the food from tearing.

Pots and pans

A good selection of pots and pans is essential for all the boiling, simmering, poaching and steaming tasks. It is worth investing in some really good, stainless steel pans. They are expensive but they will last for generations.

Frying pan

The best frying pan is made of heavy gauge, heat-conducting metal, which allows heat to be transmitted rapidly and evenly. It should have a wide flat base and shallow sides, sloping outwards to give space for lifting and turning food. A long handle makes it easier to lift.

Skimmer

A skimmer is a long-handled, shallow metal spoon. It is perforated, so when it is used to lift food, any unwanted liquid will simply drain away.

Vegetable peeler

Similar to a knife, this has two very sharp slits in it, which, when dragged along the skin of the vegetable, remove the skin. It can also be used to peel fruit.

Corer

A sharp-edged cylinder, this is used to remove the core from fruit such as apples or pears.

Pestle and mortar

A grinder and bowl, this is used for grinding herbs and spices. It can be made of ceramic, stone, wood or metal, and the insides should be rough and unglazed.

Whisk

This is an essential beating tool used to blend ingredients and incorporate air into batter or cake mixture. It is handy, too, for rescuing a lumpy sauce.

Turner

A turner, or fish slice, is an indispensable kitchen utensil for lifting and turning food, such as rashers of bacon, fried eggs, pieces of meat or fillets of fish. If it is sturdily made, preferably in stainless steel, it will last for years.

Cutting board

A plastic cutting board is easy to keep clean.

Utensils

Stainless steel steamer
Pizza cutter
Pizza slice
Colander
Olive oil canister
Garlic press
Measuring spoons
Wooden spatula
Mezzaluna

Stainless steel steamer

This is excellent for maintaining the texture and flavour of the finished dish.

Garlic press

A garlic press forces the garlic through a series of tiny holes. This also releases the oils so that the food benefits from the full flavour of the clove.

Pizza/pasta cutter

This is used for cutting pizzas or pasta. Ensure that the wheel turns freely.

Pizza slice

This is a wide-bladed slice used to help lift and transfer a pizza from the baking sheet to the plate. It is usually made of stainless steel.

Colander

This is basically a container with holes in, used for separating liquids and solids and for draining and rinsing food. It is usually made of plastic or stainless steel.

Measuring spoons

These come in sets with a tablespoon, a teaspoon, a half teaspoon, and a quarter teaspoon. They come in aluminium, plastic or stainless steel and measure both dry goods and liquids.

Spatula

Usually made of plastic, a spatula has a wide, blunt blade. It is used for moving food around a bowl and for scraping round the edges of a mixing bowl.

Oil canister

This has a long thin spout which is useful for distributing oil evenly over salads and pans.

Turning bowl

Whisk

Measuring jug

Grater

Masher

Pasta server

Rolling pin

Mezzaluna

This uses a two-handled rocking motion to chop herbs and vegetables finely.

Grater

Graters come in a box shape or a single flat sheet. They have perforations which perform different functions. The fine holes are for grating spices and rind, the medium and large holes are for grating cheese and vegetables. They are usually made of stainless steel.

Measuring jug

This is a standardized liquid measure, with a pouring lip. It is usually marked in both metric and imperial. It is available in glass, plastic or stainless steel.

Pasta server

This is a long-handled stainless steel spoon, which is used for transferring pasta from the pan. It has teeth that pick up the pasta easily and a hole which allows the liquid to drain away.

Masher

A masher is used for mashing cooked, starchy vegetables such as potatoes or swede.

Rolling pin

This is used for rolling out pasta, pastry and bread dough. It should be heavy so that it does the work, not you. It can be made of wood, plastic, nylon or marble.

Turning bowl

This has a built-in stand to support it and to prevent it slipping. It enables ease of mixing, beating or folding at different angles. The stainless steel surface is hard wearing and easy to clean.

Soups and Starters

Bacon and Turnip Soup

25 g/1 oz butter or margarine
125 g/4 oz rindless smoked bacon, coarsely chopped
1 onion, chopped
375 g/12 oz potatoes, peeled and chopped
750 g/1½ lb turnips, peeled and chopped
1.2 litres/2 pints Chicken Stock (see page 10)
1 bay leaf
1 small sprig fresh thyme or ¼ teaspoon dried thyme
150 ml/¼ pint milk
salt and freshly ground black pepper
1 tablespoon finely chopped parsley to garnish (optional)

melt the butter or margarine in a heavy-based saucepan, add the bacon and cook over a moderate heat until crisp and golden. Remove the bacon with a slotted spoon and set aside.

cook the onion, potatoes and turnips in the bacon fat for about 5 minutes over a low heat. Add the stock, bay leaf and thyme.

bring to the boil then lower the heat and cook for 30–35 minutes or until all the vegetables are soft. Remove and discard the bay leaf and sprig of thyme, if used.

purée the mixture in a blender or food processor in batches until smooth. Transfer each successive batch to a clean saucepan. Add the reserved bacon and the milk, and season with salt and pepper if necessary.

cook over a moderate heat for 35 minutes or until the soup is hot but not boiling. Stir frequently.

serve at once in heated soup plates or bowls, and sprinkle each portion with a little finely chopped parsley, if liked.

Serves 6
Preparation time: *40–45 minutes*
Cooking time: *1½ hours*

Prawn Gumbo

This Cajun soup is native to the Louisiana coast of the USA. It can be made with a variety of vegetables, meats, and seafood, but okra is its most important ingredient, as it thickens the soup and provides a luxuriously rich texture.

50 g/2 oz long-grain white rice
50 g/2 oz butter
2 garlic cloves, crushed
1 onion, chopped
1 red pepper, cored, deseeded and finely chopped
4 ripe tomatoes, skinned and chopped
¼ teaspoon cayenne pepper or more to taste
1.2 litres/2 pints Fish Stock (see page 10)
375 g/12 oz okra (vegetable), trimmed and sliced
375 g/12 oz prawns, cooked and peeled, thawed if frozen and dried on absorbent kitchen paper
1 tablespoon lime juice, freshly squeezed
salt and freshly ground black pepper

bring a large saucepan of lightly salted water to the boil. Add the rice and cook for 8–10 minutes or until tender. Drain the rice and set aside.

melt the butter in a large heavy-bottomed saucepan. Add the garlic and onion and cook gently for about 5 minutes or until soft and slightly golden. Add the red pepper and continue cooking over a moderate heat for a further 5 minutes, stirring constantly.

stir in the tomatoes and cayenne and mix well. Pour in the fish stock and bring the mixture to the boil. Add the okra, lower the heat, cover the pan and cook for 20 minutes, stirring occasionally.

add the prawns, rice and lime juice to the soup. Stir well, cover and simmer for a further 5–8 minutes. Season with salt and pepper and add a little more cayenne, if liked.

Serves 4–6
Preparation time: *20 minutes*
Cooking time: *50 minutes*

clipboard: Many recipes require skinned tomatoes – the method of skinning them is simple. Place the tomatoes in a bowl and pour over enough boiling water to cover. Leave for 1–2 minutes, then drain, cut a cross at the stem end of each tomato, and peel off the skins.

Minestrone

This is a thick, heavy Italian peasant soup, substantial enough to provide a whole meal in itself. There are numerous regional variations, depending on what combination of vegetables is chosen. Some versions are thickened with rice.

250 g/8 oz dried haricot beans, soaked overnight in water to cover

3 tablespoons olive oil

2 onions, finely chopped

2 garlic cloves, finely chopped

2 rashers streaky bacon, derinded and finely chopped

6 tomatoes, skinned (see page 20) and chopped

1.8 litres/3 pints water

600 ml/1 pint Beef Stock (see page 10)

1 tablespoon chopped marjoram

2 tablespoons tomato purée

2 carrots, peeled and diced

2 celery sticks, finely sliced

½ Savoy cabbage, finely shredded

250 g/8 oz peas, either fresh, shelled, or frozen

50 g/2 oz small pasta shapes

1 tablespoon chopped parsley

150 g/5oz Parmesan cheese, grated

salt and pepper

drain the haricot beans thoroughly in a colander then rinse under cold running water and drain again.

heat the olive oil in a large saucepan. Add the onions, garlic and bacon. Cook the mixture over a moderate heat until the onions are soft but not brown and the bacon is crisp.

stir in the tomatoes, the water and the beef stock, then add the rinsed beans, the marjoram or thyme and the tomato purée. Bring to the boil, skimming off the froth as it rises to the surface. Lower the heat and then simmer, covered, for about 2 hours or until the beans are tender.

add the carrots and celery and cook over a moderate heat for a further 15 minutes, then add the cabbage, peas and pasta. Cook for 15–18 minutes or until the vegetables and pasta are tender.

add a little more water if the soup is too thick. Add the parsley, season with salt and pepper and stir in 50 g/2 oz of the Parmesan. Serve at once in heated bowls with the remaining Parmesan served separately.

Serves 8–10
Preparation time: *about 30 minutes*, plus overnight soaking
Cooking time: *about 2¾ hours*

Tomato Chowder

Every cook should have a recipe for a fast, easily-made soup available for those occasions when time is very limited. This tasty chowder is not only easy and quick to make, it is also warming and satisfying.

1 x 300g/10 oz can condensed tomato soup
1 x 425 g/14 oz can tomatoes, sieved
1 x 325 g/11 oz can sweetcorn, drained
1 tablespoon Worcestershire sauce
3–6 drops Tabasco sauce
1 teaspoon fresh oregano, chopped, or
½ teaspoon dried oregano
½ teaspoon sugar
125 g/4 oz Cheddar cheese, grated

combine all the ingredients except the cheese in a large saucepan. Stir until thoroughly mixed.

bring to the boil over a moderate heat, stirring all the time, then lower the heat and simmer, uncovered, for 3 minutes.

ladle the soup into heated ovenproof bowls, sprinkle with the cheese and place under a preheated hot grill for 3–5 minutes until the cheese is bubbling. Serve immediately.

Serves 4–6
Preparation time: *5 minutes*
Cooking time: *about 10 minutes*

clipboard: the term 'chowder' comes from the French word *chaudière*, the name for the kettle in which the soup was cooked. This became anglicized by French settlers in the New World. The term usually refers to clam or other fish soups, but it is also used to describe other soups.

Mussel Chowder

The term 'chowder' originates from the New England seaboard of the USA. There are many recipes, but this retains the classic flavour.

2 tablespoons olive oil
250 g/8 oz streaky bacon, chopped
2 onions, finely chopped
1 celery stick, finely sliced
1 green pepper, cored, deseeded and finely chopped
450 ml/¾ pint Fish Stock (see page 10)
250 g/8 oz potatoes, peeled and diced
1 bay leaf
½ teaspoon fresh marjoram leaves, chopped, or
¼ teaspoon dried marjoram
3 tablespoons plain white flour
300 ml/½ pint milk
500 g/1 lb mussels, cooked and shelled, thawed if frozen
150 ml/¼ pint single cream
salt and white pepper
1 tablespoon finely chopped parsley, to garnish

heat the olive oil in a heavy-based saucepan and cook the bacon, uncovered, over a moderate heat until browned. Add the onions, celery and pepper and cook for 5 minutes or until the vegetables soften. Stir frequently. Add the fish stock, potatoes, bay leaf and marjoram.

bring to the boil, then lower the heat, cover the pan and simmer for 15–20 minutes or until the potatoes are tender.

blend the flour with 150 ml/¼ pint of the milk in a small bowl. Whisk the mixture into the chowder, stir until it begins to boil then slowly add the remaining milk. Add salt and pepper to taste.

lower the heat, add the mussels and simmer gently for 5 minutes, stirring from time to time. Do not allow the chowder to boil. Stir in the cream and pour the chowder into a heated soup tureen. Sprinkle the parsley over the top to garnish and serve with crusty French bread.

Serves 4–6
Preparation time: *10–15 minutes*
Cooking time: *about 30 minutes*

clipboard: Mussels are delicious but they need very careful preparation if they are to be safe. Always buy them from a reputable fishmonger. Scrub them under plenty of cold running water. Carefully remove the beards. Discard any that open at this stage. Cook in plenty of boiling water and discard any that don't open when cooked. Use the small, plump European mussels for this recipe – the large New Zealand mussels are not suitable.

Fisherman's Soup
with a hot rouille

Rouille is a piquant sauce made from an aromatic combination of garlic and pimientos. It is traditionally spread on toasted bread and served with fish soup.

I leek, chopped
2 onions, chopped
2 garlic cloves, crushed
5 tablespoons olive oil
3 tomatoes, skinned (see page 20) and chopped
2 potatoes, peeled and diced
I large red snapper or 2 medium red mullets, scaled and cleaned
I monkfish tail, skinned and filleted with the bone
750 ml/I¼ pints water
600 ml/I pint dry white wine
2 strips orange peel
I bay leaf
few sprigs of fresh fennel or thyme
½ teaspoon saffron strands (optional)
2 tablespoons chopped parsley
a little Fish Stock (see page 10) (optional)
salt and freshly ground black pepper

To garnish
French bread stick (baguette), sliced
I x quantity of Rouille (see page 8)
4 tablespoons grated Gruyère cheese

sauté the leek, onions and garlic in the olive oil until soft and golden. Add the tomatoes and potatoes and cook gently for 2–3 minutes.

remove the head of the snapper or mullets and add to the pan with the monkfish bone. Add the water, wine, orange peel, herbs and seasoning and bring to the boil. Reduce the heat, add the fish, chopped into larger pieces and simmer gently for 15 minutes.

crush the saffron, if using between your fingers and add to the pan. Stir well and continue cooking gently for 15–20 minutes. Remove and discard the fish head, fish bones, bay leaf, orange rind and herb sprigs.

pour the soup into a liquidizer or blender and blend until smooth. Return to the pan and heat through gently. Add the parsley and, if it is too thick, you can thin it down with some fish stock.

toast the slices of French bread lightly on both sides, spread with the *rouille*, sprinkle with Gruyère and serve with the hot soup.

Serves 6–8
Preparation time: *15 minutes*
Cooking time: *50–55 minutes*

Gazpacho

This iced tomato soup originates from the scorching climate of Andalusia in southern Spain. There are various recipes from all over Spain, made with slightly different combinations of fresh, raw vegetables.

1 garlic clove
1 litre/1¾ pints tomato juice
3 tablespoons olive oil
2 tablespoons lemon juice
1 tablespoon lime juice
2 teaspoons sugar
150 g/5 oz cucumber, peeled and diced
75 g/ 3 oz mild red onion or spring onions, chopped
150 g/5 oz red pepper, deseeded and diced
75 g/3 oz avocado, diced
2 tablespoons chopped mixed fresh herbs
salt and freshly ground black pepper

To serve
ice cubes
tortilla chips, coarsely crushed
lime wedges

cut the garlic clove in half and then rub the cut surfaces over the bottom and around the sides of a large mixing bowl. Discard the garlic.

pour the tomato juice into the bowl and then add the olive oil, lemon and lime juices, sugar and salt and black pepper to taste. Beat the tomato juice lightly with the other ingredients until well amalgamated.

cover the bowl with some clingfilm and chill in the refrigerator for at least 1 hour.

beat the soup again and stir in all the remaining ingredients. Place some ice cubes in individual serving bowls and pour the soup over the top. Sprinkle with coarsely crushed tortilla chips and serve with lime wedges.

Serves 6–8
Preparation time: *20 minutes*
Chilling time: *1 hour*

French Onion Soup

Onion soup is supposed to have originated in Les Halles, the Parisian food market. In fact, most countries have their own version of this heartwarming, juicy and fragrant soup.

50 g/2 oz butter
750 g/1½ lb onions, thinly sliced
2 teaspoons sugar
2 teaspoons plain flour
1 litre/1¾ pints Beef Stock (see page 10)
½ French bread stick (baguette), sliced
50 g/2 oz Gruyère cheese, grated
salt and freshly ground black pepper

melt the butter in a large saucepan and add the onions and sugar. Lower the heat to a bare simmer and cook the onions very slowly for 20–30 minutes until they are soft and a really deep golden brown. Stir occasionally and cook to a good colour without burning.

stir the flour into the onion mixture and cook over a very low heat for about 5 minutes, stirring well to prevent it burning or sticking to the bottom of the pan.

add the beef stock and the salt and freshly ground black pepper. Turn up the heat and bring to the boil, stirring all the time. Reduce the heat and simmer for 15–20 minutes. Taste the soup and add more salt and freshly ground black pepper if necessary.

toast the slices of French bread lightly on both sides in the meantime. Sprinkle with the grated Gruyère. Pour the soup into a hot tureen. Place a piece of toast in each serving bowl and ladle the hot soup over the top.

Serves 4–5
Preparation time: *15 minutes*
Cooking time: *1 hour*

Bean Soup
with Basil

250 g/8 oz French beans, sliced
250 g/8 oz fresh haricot beans, shelled (or dried haricot beans, soaked overnight and precooked for 20 minutes)
3 courgettes, sliced
4 potatoes, peeled and diced
4 tomatoes, skinned (see page 20), deseeded and chopped
2 litres/3½ pints hot water
3 garlic cloves, peeled
15 basil leaves
1½ tablespoons olive oil
250 g/8 oz shell pasta
salt and freshly ground black pepper
250 g/8 oz Parmesan or Gruyère cheese, grated, to serve

put all the beans, courgettes, potatoes and most of the chopped tomatoes in a large saucepan. Cover with hot water and season with salt and pepper. Bring to the boil, reduce the heat and simmer for 45 minutes.

pound the garlic, basil leaves and remaining tomato in a mortar in the meantime. Add the olive oil and mix well. Set aside.

add the shell pasta to the soup and continue cooking gently over low heat for a further 20 minutes, until the vegetables are cooked and tender, and the pasta shells are cooked.

put some of the reserved garlic and basil mixture into a large soup tureen or divide between 8 individual soup dishes when the soup is ready.

add a little of the soup and stir well, and then add the remaining soup. Sprinkle with grated cheese and serve with the remaining basil mixture.

Serves 8
Preparation time: *15 minutes*
Cooking time: *1 hour 5 minutes*

clipboard: Haricot beans (one of the large variety of dried beans available at supermarkets) are used widely in soups and stews, and combine particularly well with olive oil and tomatoes. They are white, fairly small and, like all dried beans, they are highly nutritious – low in carbohydrates and fat, with a high fibre content.

Savoury Soufflé Omelette

This is a starter with a difference, as it is a delicious hybrid of omelette and soufflé. Vary the flavour by using a choice of tasty fillings.

Omelette
4 eggs

water

25–50 g/1–2 oz butter

salt and freshly ground black pepper

Savoury Fillings
Cheese

3 tablespoons grated Cheddar cheese

Fish

3 tablespoons flaked shellfish, white or smoked fish, in a Béchamel Sauce (see page 8)

Meat

3 tablespoons finely diced cooked chicken, *or*

3 tablespoons finely diced ham, *or*

3 tablespoons chopped crisp bacon

Vegetables

3 tablespoons cooked mixed vegetables, in a Béchamel Sauce (see page 8)

heat the grill on a medium setting before preparing the omelette.

separate the eggs and beat the yolks with the seasoning. Add about ½ teaspoon water. Heat the butter in a large frying pan.

whisk the egg whites until they stand in peaks and fold into the yolks just before cooking.

pour the eggs into the pan and cook until set on the bottom. Place the pan under the grill (take care the handle does not get too hot). Cook until the omelette is set.

cut the omelette lightly through the centre to make it easier to fold and add the filling of your choice. Fold away from the handle and tip on to a heated plate.

Serves 2
Preparation time: *5 minutes, plus filling*
Cooking time: *4–5 minutes*

Cheese Soufflé

50 g/2 oz butter
50 g/2 oz plain flour
250 ml/8 fl oz milk
2 tablespoons single cream
4 egg yolks
150 g/5 oz Gruyère cheese, grated
¼ teaspoon freshly grated nutmeg
5 egg whites
salt and freshly ground white pepper

butter a 1.2 litre/2 pint soufflé dish or two 600 ml/1 pint dishes.

make a white sauce: melt the butter in a saucepan and stir in the flour. Cook for 1–2 minutes over low heat and then gradually add the milk, stirring well between each addition until the sauce is thick and smooth.

cook very gently for 15 minutes stirring constantly with a wooden spoon. Remove from the heat and stir in the cream.

stir the egg yolks into the sauce, a little at a time. Add the Gruyère, salt, pepper and nutmeg to taste. Beat well until the cheese melts and the mixture is really smooth.

whisk the egg whites in a clean bowl until they are really stiff, but not dry. Fold them gently into the cheese sauce mixture with a metal spoon using a figure of eight motion.

transfer the mixture to the soufflé dish or dishes. Bake in a preheated oven, 180°C/350°F/Gas Mark 4, for 15 minutes. Increase the temperature to 200°C/400°F/Gas Mark 6 and cook for a further 15 minutes until the soufflé is well risen and golden. Serve immediately.

Serves 4
Preparation time: *20 minutes*
Cooking time: *30 minutes*
Oven temperature: *180°C/350°F/Gas Mark 4,*
then *200°C/400°F/Gas Mark 6*

clipboard: To test if a soufflé is cooked, push a metal skewer down into the centre – if it comes out clean, the soufflé is cooked. The soufflé is much better-tasting if it is slightly moist inside, so do not leave it in the oven longer than instructed. Soufflés are not difficult to cook – the main reason that problems may arise is if they are not served straight from the oven to the table. So make sure that everyone is seated and ready to eat.

Pâté de Campagne

This is one of an infinite variety of country pâté recipes found all over France. Each region has its speciality, handed down over generations. This version is moist, tender and deliciously flavoured.

50 g/2 oz butter, plus a little extra for greasing
2 onions, finely chopped
4 garlic cloves, crushed
500 g/1 lb pig's liver, diced
275 g/9 oz rindless streaky bacon rashers
500 g/1 lb lean pork, minced or chopped
2 tablespoons chopped parsley
½ teaspoon dried sage
¼ teaspoon ground mace
¼ teaspoon ground nutmeg
2 egg whites
2 tablespoons brandy
2 bay leaves
salt and freshly ground black pepper

grease a 500 g/1 lb terrine or loaf tin lightly.

melt the butter in a frying pan and sauté the onions and garlic gently for a few minutes until tender and golden. Transfer to a large bowl. Add the liver to the pan and fry until lightly browned. Remove and mince or chop.

chop 200 g/7 oz of the streaky bacon and add to the bowl with the liver, pork, parsley, sage, mace, nutmeg, salt and pepper, egg whites and brandy. Mix together well until thoroughly combined.

line the terrine or loaf tin with the remaining bacon rashers so that they hang over the sides. Fill with the pâté mixture and fold the bacon over the top. Put the 2 bay leaves on top and place in a roasting pan of hot water.

cook in a preheated oven, 190°C/375°F/Gas Mark 5, for 1½ hours or until the juices run clear and the pâté has shrunk from the sides of the tin.

leave the pâté to cool for 30 minutes then cover with a piece of greaseproof paper or kitchen foil and weigh it down with some light weights. Leave until completely cold and set. If you like, you can replace the bay leaves with fresh ones. Cover and refrigerate for about 36 hours. Serve sliced with toast or crusty bread.

Serves 8
Preparation time: *30 minutes*
Cooking time: *1½ hours*
Oven temperature: *190°C/375°F/Gas Mark 5*

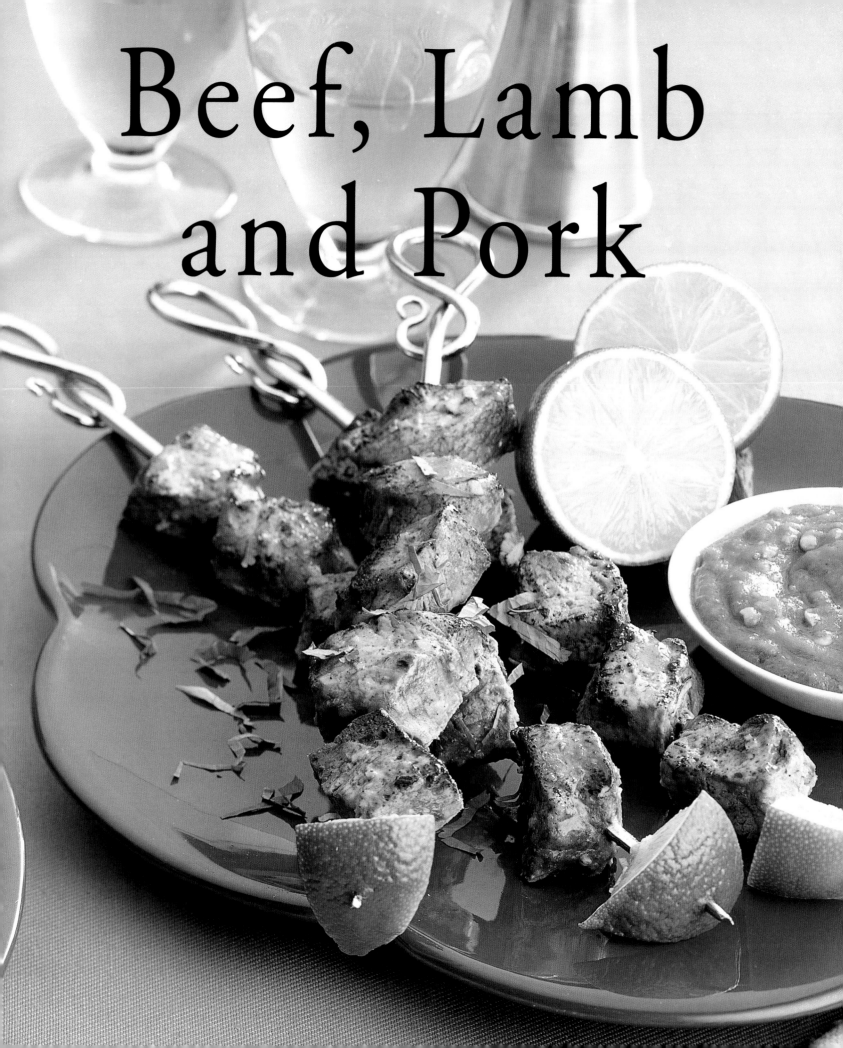

Beef, Lamb and Pork

Pot-Roast of Beef

4 tablespoons vegetable oil

25 g/1 oz butter

1.25–1.5 kg/2½–3 lb topside or
silverside of beef

2 large onions, quartered

2 large carrots, peeled and cut into
1 cm/½ inch slices

1 *bouquet garni* or 2 sprigs each thyme,
parsley and marjoram

4 black peppercorns

½ teaspoon salt

150 ml/¼ pint red wine mixed with
450 ml/¾ pint water

2 teaspoons cornflour

heat the oil and butter in a flameproof casserole, add the beef and turn until browned.

reduce the heat and pack the vegetables all round the beef. Add the herbs, peppercorns and salt. Pour in the wine and water.

cover the casserole closely with foil, then the lid and cook in a preheated oven, 150°C/300°F/Gas Mark 2, for 3 hours until the beef is tender and cooked through.

transfer the beef to a heated serving dish. Discard the herbs. Lift out the vegetables with a perforated spoon and place round the beef. Keep hot while making the sauce.

bring the cooking liquid in the casserole to the boil. Mix the cornflour with a little water to make a smooth paste, pour a little of the boiling gravy on to it, stirring well and pour back into the boiling gravy in the casserole, stirring constantly. If the sauce is too thick, thin with a little stock or water and return to the boil. Pour the sauce over the beef and vegetables and serve.

Serves 6
Preparation time: *30 minutes*
Cooking time: *3 hours 20 minutes*
Oven temperature: *150°C/300°F/Gas Mark 2*

clipboard: Economical joints of beef such as topside, silverside or brisket are ideal for this slow, gentle method of pot-roasting, which breaks down the tough fibres, and results in a tender, succulent, well-flavoured joint. In fact the meat is being cooked in the steam from the liquid ingredients, rather than roasted in the conventional manner.

Satay Lembu

These barbecued skewers of succulent beef are full of the flavour of Malayan cooking. Satay represents two major cultural influences in the cuisine – the kebab from the Arab world, and the sauce from India.

500–625 g/1–1¼ lb rump steak

Coconut milk
125g/4 oz fresh coconut or 50 g/2 oz desiccated coconut
300 ml/½ pint water

Marinade
2 garlic cloves
pinch of ground cardamom
pinch of ground cinnamon
pinch of ground cumin
pinch of curry powder
2 teaspoons ginger, chopped
freshly ground black pepper

To garnish
lime wedges
few sprigs parsley

To serve
Satay Sauce (see page 9)

pour the prepared coconut milk (see clipboard below) into a container. Peel and crush the garlic, and add to the coconut milk with the other marinade ingredients.

cut the steak into neat 2–5 cm/1–2 inch pieces. Put into the marinade and leave for several hours.

thread the meat on to bamboo sticks or long metal skewers. Drain well and cook under a preheated grill or over a barbecue fire. Make sure the barbecue is well heated.

garnish with wedges of lime, sprigs of parsley and serve with rice, the satay sauce and a crisp salad.

Serves 4
Preparation time: *10 minutes, plus 5–10 hours marinating*
Cooking time: *20–25 minutes*

clipboard: There are various ways to make coconut milk. Grate the fresh coconut and put it into a bowl. Alternatively, put the desiccated coconut in a bowl. Boil the water, pour over the coconut and leave for several hours. Strain through a fine sieve, and use as required. For a quicker method: put the fresh coconut and water into a liquidizer and blend until smooth. This gives a thick mixture that can be diluted with more water, or you can use only half the quantity of coconut.

Braised Beef
with cheese dumplings

25 g/1 oz beef dripping or oil
2 onions, sliced
750 g/1½ lb stewing beef, cubed
1 rounded tablespoon plain flour
1 teaspoon brown sugar
1 pinch of cinnamon
300 ml/½ pint brown ale
salt and freshly ground black pepper

Dumplings
125g/4 oz self-raising flour
50 g/2 oz suet, shredded, or margarine, melted
25 g/1 oz Cheddar cheese, grated
2–3 tablespoons water
salt and freshly ground black pepper

heat the fat or oil in a frying pan, cook the onions until soft, then transfer into a casserole. Brown the beef quickly on all sides in the pan, then add the flour and let it cook for 1 minute, stirring from time to time.

add the sugar and cinnamon and gradually pour in the brown ale. Stir well, then add salt and pepper to taste.

put the meat and gravy into the casserole, cover, and cook in a preheated oven, 180°C/350°F/Gas Mark 4 for 30 minutes. Then reduce the oven temperature to 160°C/325°F/Gas Mark 3, and continue cooking for 1 further hour.

make the dumplings next. Mix the dry ingredients together, season and add the water gradually. Add a little more if needed to make a fairly slack dough. Flour the hands and break the dough into 8 small pieces, then roll into little balls with the palms of the hands. Chill until required.

test the meat with a fork after 1½ hours cooking time. If necessary, cook for a further 30 minutes. If the casserole is dry, add some water or beer.

place the dumplings on top of the casserole about 20 minutes before the meat is ready, leave off the lid and cook until they are risen, about 20–30 minutes. Alternatively, poach the dumplings about 4 at a time in a saucepan of boiling salted water for about 15 minutes. Drain well.

Serves 4–6
Preparation time: *30 minutes*
Cooking time: *about 2 hours*
Oven temperature: *180°C/350°F/Gas Mark 4*, then *160°C/325°F/GasMark 3*

Beef Stroganoff

This is still one of the most popular 'special occasion' dishes, and requires good quality, tender meat. This makes a delicious sauce with the sour cream stirred into the meat juices.

3 onions, finely chopped
50 g/2 oz butter
250 g/8 oz button mushrooms, thinly sliced
1 green pepper, deseeded and cut in fine strips
500g/1 lb fillet or good rump steak, cut into strips 5cm/2 in long, 5 mm/¼ inch thick
150 ml/¼ pint double dairy soured cream
salt and freshly ground pepper
1 teaspoon chopped parsley, to garnish

fry the onions in half the butter in a large deep frying pan until pale gold. Add the mushrooms and green pepper to the pan and cook for 5 minutes. Remove the onions, mushrooms and green pepper from the pan.

melt the remaining butter and heat, then fry the meat for about 4 minutes, turning it so it becomes evenly cooked.

return the onions, mushrooms and peppers to the pan, season well, stir in the soured cream and blend well. Heat until piping hot but do not allow to boil. Garnish with chopped parsley.

Serves 4
Preparation time: *10 minutes*
Cooking time: *15 minutes*

clipboard: A rather more economical version of this dish can be made by using a cheaper cut of meat such as braising steak. Cut the meat into strips as above, and marinate it in lemon juice overnight to tenderize it.

Lamb Casserole
with red wine and herbs

1.25kg/2½ lb shoulder of lamb (trimmed weight), boned and cubed

1 large onion, finely chopped

2 garlic cloves, crushed

2 large tomatoes, skinned (see page 20), deseeded and quartered

1 *bouquet garni* including thyme, parsley, rosemary, marjoram and bayleaf

rind of 1 orange, cut into thin strips

1 bottle of dry red wine

2 tablespoons olive oil

250 g/8 oz rindless streaky bacon, diced

300 ml/½ pint Chicken Stock (see page 10)

250 g/8 oz plain flour

salt and freshly ground black pepper

75 g/3 oz small black olives, to serve

1 tablespoon chopped parsley, to garnish

trim any excess fat from the cubed lamb. Put the meat in a large casserole dish with the onion, garlic, tomatoes, *bouquet garni*, orange rind, salt and 1 teaspoon pepper. Pour the wine over the top, add the oil and stir well. Cover and leave to marinate in the refrigerator for 4 hours.

blanch the bacon in boiling water for 2 minutes and drain. Add to the casserole with the chicken stock so that the lamb is well covered with liquid. Season with a pinch of salt.

mix the flour with a little water to form a paste, then roll into a thin strip. Press the paste between the casserole dish and lid to form a seal.

cook in a preheated oven, 200°C/400°F/Gas Mark 6, for 1 hour, then reduce the temperature to 180°C/350°F/Gas Mark 4 and cook for a further 2 hours. Discard the strip of flour paste and remove the *bouquet garni*.

sprinkle the casserole with black olives and garnish with parsley. Serve with plain boiled rice.

Serves 4–6
Preparation time: *15 minutes, plus 4 hours marinating*
Cooking time: *3 hours*
Oven temperature: *200°C/400°F/Gas Mark 6,* then *180°C/350°F/Gas Mark 4*

Rack of Lamb

2 lean best ends of neck of lamb, chined
750g/1½ lb courgettes
1 x 200 g/7 oz can sweetcorn, drained
75 g/3 oz fresh wholemeal breadcrumbs
rind, finely grated, and juice of 1 small orange
4 tablespoons Quark cheese or skimmed milk soft cheese
375 g/12 oz baby sweetcorn cobs
1 tablespoon soya or sunflower oil
salt and freshly ground black pepper
rosemary sprigs, to garnish

remove the skin and most of the fat from the surface of the meat, leaving just a thin, even layer of fat. Cut away the meat from the top 3.5 cm/1½ inches of the rib ends and scrape them well. Using a sharp knife, score the surface of the fat in a diamond pattern.

grate 250 g/8 oz of the courgettes by hand or in a food processor and mix with the sweetcorn, breadcrumbs, orange rind and Quark or skimmed milk soft cheese. Season the mixture with salt and pepper.

shape the mixture into a long roll and place this along the curve of the bones of one joint; place the other joint over the first so that the bones interlock, forming 'crossed swords'. Tie them firmly with string and wrap the tops of the bones with aluminium foil to prevent them burning.

place the joint on a rack in a roasting tin. Place in a preheated oven, 180°C/350°F/Gas Mark 4, and cook for 1¼ hours until the lamb is just tender and still slightly pink in the centre.

cut the remaining courgettes into long sticks about the size of the baby corn cobs in the meantime. Place the courgettes and corn cobs in a pan with the oil and the orange juice. Sprinkle them with pepper and cover the pan tightly. Cook over a fairly high heat, shaking the pan occasionally until the vegetables are just tender.

remove the meat from the oven and skim any fat from the juices. Place the meat in the centre of a warmed platter and arrange the vegetables around it. Garnish with sprigs of rosemary. Mix the cooking juices and serve separately as a sauce.

Serves 6
Preparation time: *40–50 minutes*
Cooking time: *1¼ hours*
Oven temperature: *180°C/350°F/Gas Mark 4*

Flour, Grains and Rice

Popcorn

Couscous

Buckwheat flour

Pinhead oatmeal

Cornflour

Rye flakes

Popcorn

This is the dried kernels of sweetcorn which, when heated in oil, pop to form a fluffy corn snack. It can be coated with sugar or salt.

Buckwheat flour

This flour is made from roasted buckwheat seeds and is used in pancakes, blinis, crisp thin cakes and Asian soya noodles. The seeds came originally from central Asia, but the buckwheat plant is, in fact, a native of the Soviet Union.

Cornflour

A fine white flour, this is sometimes known as corn starch. It is made from corn kernels and is used in cooking to thicken sauces, gravies and puddings, and to make blancmange.

Rye flakes

Also known as rolled rye, rye flakes are cultivated to make flour and for distilling into whisky. They are also used in soups and casseroles.

Couscous

A pasta made from durum wheat and semolina, this is a staple in North African cooking. To cook couscous, soak it in boiling water, fluff it up with a fork and add a knob of butter or a little oil. Couscous is a good accompaniment to meat, fish and vegetable dishes.

Pinhead oatmeal

Also referred to as fine oatmeal, this has been finely ground so that it can be used in pancakes, oatcakes and muffins.

Wild rice

This is not, in fact, rice but the seeds of an aquatic grass that is native to the

Basmati rice

Soya flour

Plain flour

Wholemeal flour

Wild rice

Polenta

Minnesota Lakes in the US. It is surrounded by a tough husk which is long and dark brown and, when the husk is cooked, it bursts open to reveal a pale interior that can be boiled or steamed. Wild rice has a distinctive earthy flavour and is served as an accompaniment to fish, poultry or vegetables.

Basmati rice

A rice native to Asia, this is widely associated with Indian cuisine. Basmati rice should always be soaked before cooking.

Polenta

A thick porridge of cornmeal, water and butter, polenta can be eaten hot with Parmesan as a vegetarian dish, or it can be served either with chopped meat or with a sauce.

Soya flour

This is made from ground, roasted soya beans. It is rich in protein and carbohydrates. The bread made from it is rather sweet.

Wholemeal flour

This is a coarse-textured flour which can be used to make bread, cakes, biscuits and pasta. The flour is made by grinding the wheat kernel which includes the bran, the germ, and the endosperm. Wholemeal flour is particularly popular with health-conscious eaters, because of its high fibre content.

Plain flour

After the flour has been ground, the germ and bran are removed, and the flour is bleached to remove the colour. White flour is used in the great majority of baking recipes.

Catalan Pork Stew
with tomatoes and aubergines

150 ml/¼ pint olive oil

750g/1½ lb lean pork cut into 2.5 cm/1 inch cubes

1 large onion, sliced

2 garlic cloves, crushed

500 g/1 lb tomatoes, skinned (see page 20) and chopped

1 green pepper, deseeded and chopped

1½ teaspoons paprika

150 ml/¼ pint Chicken Stock (see page 10)

1 aubergine, sliced

2–3 tablespoons seasoned flour

salt and freshly ground black pepper

1 tablespoon chopped coriander leaves, to garnish

heat 2 tablespoons of the oil in a large saucepan or flameproof casserole, add the pork and sauté gently until golden brown on all sides, turning occasionally. Remove from the pan with a slotted spoon.

add the onion and garlic and cook until soft and golden. Return the meat to the pan and stir in the tomatoes, green pepper, paprika and stock. Season with salt and freshly ground black pepper.

bring to the boil, cover with greaseproof paper and a lid and simmer gently for 1 hour or until the meat is tender.

dip the aubergine slices in seasoned flour. Heat some of the remaining oil in a large frying pan. When it is hot, fry the aubergine slices, a few at a time, until they are golden brown on both sides. Add more oil as required.

remove with a slotted spoon and pat dry with kitchen paper. Serve with the fried aubergine, scattered with coriander, and plain boiled rice.

Serves 4
Preparation time: *20 minutes*
Cooking time: *1¼ hours*

clipboard: If you dislike the slightly bitter taste of aubergines and wish to remove it, you can prepare them as follows. Sprinkle the slices with salt and leave for 20–30 minutes. Drain, rinse in cold water and dry on kitchen paper. They are now ready to use.

Stir-Fried Beef
with baby corn and red peppers

1 tablespoon Szechuan pepper

3 tablespoons vegetable oil

500 g/1 lb rump or fillet steak, cut into thin strips across the grain

2 fresh green chillies, deseeded and finely chopped

1 onion, thinly sliced

1 red pepper, cored, deseeded and cut lengthways into thin strips

1 x 425 g/14 oz can baby sweetcorn, drained

Sauce

3 tablespoons soy sauce

2 tablespoons Chinese wine or dry sherry

1 tablespoon dark soft brown sugar

1 teaspoon five spice powder

heat a wok until hot, add the pepper and dry-fry over a gentle heat for 1–2 minutes. Remove from the wok, crush in a mortar, and set aside.

prepare the sauce: put all the ingredients in a bowl or jug and stir well to mix. Set aside.

heat the wok again until hot. Add 2 tablespoons of the oil and heat over a moderate heat until hot. Add the beef strips, chillies and crushed peppercorns, increase the heat to high and stir-fry for 3–4 minutes or until the beef is browned on all sides. Remove the wok from the heat and tip the beef and its juices into a bowl. Set aside.

return the wok to a moderate heat, add the remaining oil and heat until hot. Add the onion and red pepper and stir-fry for 2–3 minutes or until softened slightly, then add the baby sweetcorn and stir-fry for 1–2 minutes or until hot.

return the beef and its juices to the wok, pour in the sauce and increase the heat to high. Toss for 2–3 minutes or until all the ingredients are combined and piping hot. Serve at once.

Serves 2–3 as a main dish or 4 as part of an Oriental meal
Preparation time: *20–30 minutes*
Cooking time: *9–12 minutes*

clipboard: Szechuan pepper is not, in fact, pepper but is made from the seed casings of a species of prickly ash that grows in the Szechuan province of Western China. Cultivated in the lush, almost tropical climate, it has a superb pungent flavour. It can be bought in Oriental food stores, and is one of the ingredients in Chinese five spice powder.

Roast Beef

with individual Yorkshire puddings

1 roasting joint of beef
Dijon or French mustard
freshly ground black pepper

Yorkshire Pudding

125 g/4 oz plain flour
pinch of salt
1 large egg
300 ml/½ pint milk, or milk and water
margarine or lard for greasing

check the weight of the joint, and calculate cooking time. If the joint has a bone – e.g. rib of beef – allow 1–2 minutes less per 500 g/1 lb. Place the meat in a roasting tin, season with pepper and coat with mustard.

fast-roasting method: preheat the oven to 220°C/425°F/Gas Mark 7. Allow 15 minutes per 500 g/1 lb plus 15 minutes for rare beef; 20 minutes per 500 g/1 lb plus 20 minutes for medium-cooked beef; 25 minutes per 500 g/1 lb plus 25 minutes for well-cooked beef. Reduce the heat to 190°C/375°F/Gas Mark 5 after the first hour's cooking.

slow-roasting method: Preheat the oven to 180°C/350°F/Gas Mark 4. Allow 25 minutes per 500 g/1 lb plus 25 minutes for medium-cooked beef; 35 minutes per 500 g/1 lb plus 35 minutes over for well-cooked beef. Reduce the heat to 160°C/325°F/Gas Mark 3 after 1½ hours. (Slow-roasting is not recommended for cooking rare beef.)

make the Yorkshire puddings: blend the flour, salt, egg and milk or milk and water to make a batter. Whisk just before cooking.

remove the beef from the oven and heat to 230° C/450°F/Gas Mark 8. Grease a deep patty tin, heat well and put in the batter. Cook for 10–12 minutes until well risen. Reduce the oven temperature to the original setting. Return the meat. Continue cooking for 8–15 minutes at the higher temperature or 15–20 minutes at the lower temperature. Remove the meat and pudding. Transfer to a serving dish, and serve with gravy made from the meat juices.

Makes: *12 Yorkshire puddings*
Preparation time: *20–25 minutes*
Cooking time and oven
temperature: *see above*

Beef Tacos

These fried, stuffed tortillas are a favourite fast food in Mexico. They are deservedly popular, and people who like fresh, spicy flavours will find them quite irresistible.

500 g/1 lb steak, minced
75 g/3 oz onion, chopped
65 g/2½ oz green pepper, deseeded and chopped
1 garlic clove, crushed
1 teaspoon dried oregano
½ teaspoon hot paprika
¼ teaspoon ground cumin
¼ teaspoon dried hot red chilli pepper flakes
125 ml/4 fl oz tomato purée
12 tortillas
oil for frying
salt and freshly ground black pepper

To serve
1 lettuce, shredded
2 tomatoes, finely chopped
2 tablespoons Cheddar cheese, grated
1 avocado, diced
150 ml/¼ pint sour cream
Salsa Cruda (see page 9)

cook the minced steak in a frying pan until brown and crumbly, stirring occasionally and breaking it up with a wooden spoon.

add the onion, green pepper and garlic and cook, stirring occasionally, until softened. Stir in the herbs, spices and seasoning to taste.

add the tomato purée and mix well. Cover and cook gently for 10 minutes, stirring occasionally.

place a little of the mixture on each tortilla and roll up. Secure with a cocktail stick and then fry quickly in a little oil until golden. Serve with the various accompaniments.

Serves 4–6
Preparation time: *15 minutes*
Cooking time: *30 minutes*

clipboard: Tortillas are thin pancakes made from unleavened cornmeal. They are now available in larger supermarkets and are sold in packets in ready-to-cook form.

Beef Bourguignon

This is one of the great dishes of French regional cooking, in which the long, slow cooking releases the flavours of the meat, garlic and wine. Use the best Burgundy you can afford, to achieve the most authentic result.

1 large onion, thinly sliced
a few parsley sprigs
a few thyme sprigs
1 bay leaf, crumbled
1 kg/2 lb chuck steak or top rump cut into 2.5 cm/1 inch cubes
2 tablespoons marc or brandy
400 ml/14 fl oz red Burgundy wine
2 tablespoons olive oil
50 g/2 oz butter
150 g/5 oz lean bacon, roughly chopped
24 small pickling onions, peeled
500 g/1 lb button mushrooms, halved
25 g/1 oz plain flour
300 ml/½ pint Beef Stock (see page 10)
1 garlic clove, crushed
1 *bouquet garni*
salt and freshly ground black pepper

put a few onion slices in a deep bowl with a little parsley, thyme and some crumbled bay leaf. Place a few pieces of beef on top and continue layering up in this way until all the onion, beef and herbs are used. Mix together the marc or brandy with the wine and oil and pour over the beef. Cover and leave to marinate for at least 4 hours.

melt the butter in a flameproof casserole, add the bacon and fry over moderate heat until golden brown. Remove and set aside. Add the small onions and fry until golden on all sides. Add the mushrooms and fry, stirring, for 1 minute. Drain and set aside.

remove the beef from the marinade then strain the marinade and set aside. Add the beef to the casserole and fry briskly until browned on all sides. Sprinkle in the flour and cook, stirring, for 1 minute. Gradually stir in the strained marinade then add the stock, garlic and *bouquet garni*. Season to taste, cover and simmer gently for 2 hours.

skim off any fat on the surface, add the bacon, onions and mushrooms to the casserole. Cover and simmer for 30 minutes or until the beef is tender. Discard the *bouquet garni* and serve immediately.

Serves 4–6
Preparation time: *30 minutes, plus 4 hours marinating*
Cooking time: *2½ hours*

Steak, Kidney and Oyster Pudding

Pastry

250 g/8 oz suet, shredded
500 g/1 lb plain flour
50 g/2 oz fresh white breadcrumbs
pinch of salt
300 ml/½ pint cold water

Filling

2 tablespoons plain flour, seasoned
1.5 kg/3 lb rump steak trimmed and cut
into 2.5 cm/1 inch cubes
500 g/1 lb ox kidney, chopped
1 small onion, grated
2 teaspoons Worcestershire sauce
2 teaspoons chopped parsley
6 oysters, fresh or canned
600 ml/1 pint Beef Stock (see page 10)
salt and freshly ground black pepper

grease a 2.3 litre/4 pint pudding basin. Make the pastry: mix together all the dry ingredients then add the water slowly, to make a smooth, pliable dough.

turn on to a floured surface and roll out. Reserve enough to cover the top. Cut a strip long enough to line the basin sides, plus a round for the bottom. Press to seal the edges.

sift the flour on to a flat plate then roll the meat and onion in it and put into the lined basin.

add salt, pepper, Worcestershire sauce, parsley and oysters and mix in carefully. Add the stock, which should not come higher than 2.5 cm/1 inch from the top. Roll out the remaining suet crust to fit the top. Moisten the edge and lay it on, pressing down at the rim.

cover with buttered greaseproof paper or aluminium foil pleated across the middle to allow the pudding to rise. Tie securely and stand in the top of a steamer or else in a deep saucepan.

pour in boiling water. If the pudding is in a saucepan do not let the water come above the rim of the basin. Put the lid on the saucepan or steamer and cook for 4–5 hours, topping up the water as necessary. Longer cooking will only improve the pudding. To serve, remove the paper or foil and wrap the basin in a napkin or folded tea towel.

Serves 6–8
Preparation time: *45 minutes*
Cooking time: *5 hours*

Fillet Steak

baked in pastry

40 g/1½ oz butter
1 tablespoon oil
2 small onions, finely chopped
1 garlic clove, crushed
125 g/4 oz mushrooms, finely chopped
pinch of ground nutmeg
4 fillet steaks, about 175 g/6 oz each, trimmed
250 g/8 oz frozen puff pastry
1 tablespoon plain flour for rolling out
1 egg, beaten
4 slices ham
salt and freshly ground black pepper
fresh chervil or parsley sprigs, to garnish

heat 25 g/1 oz of the butter and the oil in a frying pan and gently cook the onions and garlic until soft. Add the mushrooms, salt, pepper and nutmeg and stir over a gentle heat.

heat the remaining butter in a clean frying pan, add the fillet steaks and then sear quickly on both sides. Remove from the pan, cool quickly and keep chilled until required.

roll out the pastry on a lightly floured surface and cut into 8 rounds large enough to half cover the steaks. Brush a 2.5 cm/1 inch border around the edge of each pastry round with beaten egg. Cut the ham into 8 rounds the same size as the steaks.

place one piece of ham on each of 4 pastry rounds. Cover the ham with a portion of the mushroom mixture, a fillet steak, another portion of mushrooms and another round of ham. Top with a pastry circle. Seal the edges of the pastry between your fingers and then with a fork.

cut any pastry trimmings into leaves and use to decorate. Brush with beaten egg and cook in a preheated oven, 220°C/425°F/Gas Mark 7, for 20 minutes until golden brown. Serve with chervil or parsley sprigs.

Serves 4
Preparation time: *30 minutes*
Cooking time: *30–35 minutes*
Oven temperature: *220°C/425°F/Gas Mark 7*

Fish and Shellfish

Sole Véronique

4 medium sole, skinned and filleted
450 ml/¾ pint water
1 small shallot or onion (optional)
1 parsley sprig
150 ml/¼ pint white wine
125 g/4 oz black or white grapes, skinned and deseeded
salt and freshly ground white pepper

Cream sauce
25 g/1 oz butter
20 g/¾ oz flour
150 ml/¼ pint double cream

To garnish
few extra grapes, deseeded (optional)
fennel or dill leaves

ask the fishmonger for the heads and skins of the fish to make a stock if he prepares the fish for you, or reserve them if you do it yourself. Make a stock: put fish trimmings and water into a saucepan. Peel the shallot or onion but leave it whole and add to the pan with a little seasoning and the parsley. Cover and simmer steadily for 20 minutes. Strain the stock – you need 225 ml/7½ fl oz. Add this to the white wine.

put one or two skinned and deseeded grapes on each fillet of sole before rolling up tightly. Secure the rolls with fine wooden cocktail sticks. Put them into an oblong casserole and cover with the stock; add any remaining skinned and deseeded grapes. Cover and cook in a preheated oven, 200°C/400°F/Gas Mark 6, for 25 minutes or until tender.

lift the fish rolls and grapes from the stock; remove the cocktail sticks from the rolls. Place the fish on a heated dish, cover with kitchen foil so it does not dry and keep hot. Strain and reserve the liquid from the casserole.

make the sauce: heat the butter in a pan, stir in the flour, then blend in 225 ml/7½ fl oz of the reserved liquid. Stir as the sauce thickens, then gradually blend in the cream and any extra seasoning required. Heat gently without boiling, then add the skinned grapes. Spoon the sauce with the grapes on to heated plates. Arrange the fish rolls on top. Garnish with a few extra grapes if liked — deseeded but not skinned — and the fennel or dill leaves. Serve with crisp mangetout and new potatoes.

Serves: 4
Preparation time: *25 minutes (55 minutes if you prepare the fish yourself)*
Cooking time: *50 minutes*
Oven temperature: *200°C/400°F/Gas Mark 6*

clipboard: To skin grapes, place them in a bowl and cover with boiling water. Leave for 1–2 minutes, drain, cut a cross at the stem end of each grape, and peel off the skin.

Classic Fish Pie

1 kg/2 lb potatoes, peeled and cut into chunks
750 g/1½ lb cod, hake or haddock, skinned, filleted
and cut into 4 equal pieces
900 ml/1½ pints milk
75 g/3 oz butter
40 g/1½ oz plain flour
salt and freshly ground black pepper
1 tablespoon chopped chives, to garnish

boil the potatoes in a large saucepan of salted water for about 15–20 minutes or until tender.

arrange the pieces of fish in a dish in 2 layers while the potatoes are cooking. Season with salt and pepper and pour over 750 ml/1¼ pints of the milk. Cover closely with kitchen foil and bake in a preheated oven at 180°C/350°F/Gas Mark 4 for 25 minutes.

drain the potatoes and pass them through a mouli légumes or sieve. Add 40 g/1½ oz of the butter and 150 ml/¼ pint of the milk and beat until soft and creamy. Set aside to cool but do not chill.

melt 25 g/1 oz of the butter in a medium saucepan just before removing the fish from the oven, sprinkle in the flour and cook, stirring, for 1–2 minutes. Remove from the heat. Strain the cooking liquid from the fish and gradually stir into the butter and flour mixture. Return to the heat and cook, stirring, for 2–3 minutes. Season to taste.

pour the sauce evenly over the fish and leave to cool completely.

spoon the potato over the fish, lightly smooth the surface then mark the top in a pattern with a fork. Dot with the remaining butter. Bake on the top shelf of the preheated oven, 180°C/350°F/Gas Mark 4, for about 25 minutes until the fish is heated through and the topping is browned. Serve garnished with the chopped chives.

Serves: 4
Preparation time: *15 minutes, plus cooling*
Cooking time: *50 minutes*
Oven temperature: *180°C/350°F/Gas Mark 4*

clipboard: For a richer pie, stir 2 tablespoons of double cream into the sauce just before pouring it over the fish.

Bouillabaisse

This sumptuous fish stew from the south of France is generally recognized as having originated in Marseilles, though various recipes can be found throughout Provence.

200 ml/⅓ pint olive oil

2 onions, thinly sliced

2 leeks, trimmed and thinly sliced

3 tomatoes, skinned (see page 20), deseeded and chopped

4 garlic cloves, crushed

1 fennel sprig

1 thyme sprig

1 bay leaf

1 strip orange rind without pith

750 g/1½ lb shellfish e.g. crab, mussels, king prawns

2 litres/3½ pints boiling water

2.5 kg/5 lb mixed fish e.g. John Dory, monkfish, sea bass, skinned and filleted

4 pinches of saffron powder

salt and freshly ground black pepper

To serve

slices of hot toast made from French bread

250 ml/8 fl oz Rouille (see page 8)

heat the olive oil in a large saucepan, add the onions, leeks, chopped tomatoes and garlic and sauté over low heat for a few minutes until soft, stirring frequently. Stir in the fennel, thyme, bay leaf and orange rind.

add the shellfish, boiling water and some salt and freshly ground black pepper to the pan. Turn up the heat and boil for about 3 minutes to allow the oil and water to amalgamate.

add whatever fish you are using to the saucepan and reduce the heat. Continue cooking the fish over medium heat for 12–15 minutes until cooked. The flesh should be opaque and tender but still firm – it should not be falling apart.

taste the bouillabaisse when the fish is cooked, and adjust the seasoning. Stir in the saffron, then pour into a warmed tureen or soup dishes.

serve immediately with slices of hot toasted French bread topped with a spoonful of rouille.

Serves: 6–8
Preparation time: *20 minutes*
Cooking time: *30 minutes*

Red Snapper
with limes and coriander

The fresh, tangy taste of limes and coriander gives an exciting, aromatic New World flavouring to fish cooked in this exuberant Mexican style.

1 kg/2 lb red snapper or other white fish, skinned and filleted

4 tablespoons lime or lemon juice

2 teaspoons salt

4 tablespoons olive oil

25 g/1 oz fresh breadcrumbs

1 garlic clove, crushed

6 tablespoons finely chopped coriander leaves

1 teaspoon grated lime or lemon rind

freshly ground black pepper

warmed tortillas, to serve (optional)

rinse the fish fillets under running cold water and pat dry with absorbent kitchen paper. Rub the fish with half of the lime or lemon juice and 1 teaspoon of the salt, and place skin side down in a lightly oiled, heavy-bottomed frying pan.

add enough cold water to cover the fish and then simmer gently over low heat for 5 minutes, turning twice during the cooking time.

heat half of the olive oil in another pan, and add the breadcrumbs, garlic, the remaining salt and 4 tablespoons of the coriander. Cook over low heat, stirring constantly, until the crumbs are golden brown. Spread over the fish and simmer for 7–10 minutes until the fish flakes easily.

blend the remaining lime or lemon juice and oil together and pour over the fish. Cook for 2–3 minutes. Combine the remaining coriander with the grated lime or lemon rind and sprinkle over the fish. Season with black pepper and serve hot with warmed tortillas if you want an authentic Mexican touch.

Serves: 4
Preparation time: *10 minutes*
Cooking time: *20 minutes*

Spicy Fish Stew
with peppers, limes and chillies

3 tablespoons olive oil

I large onion, chopped

2 garlic cloves, crushed

I large red pepper, deseeded and chopped

I large yellow pepper, deseeded and chopped

500 g/I lb tomatoes, skinned (see page 20) and chopped

2 tablespoons finely chopped fresh root ginger

I tablespoon chopped fresh coriander

2 teaspoons chopped oregano

rind of I lime, grated

few drops of hot chilli sauce

2–4 dried red chillies, chopped

1.2 kg/2½ lb monkfish, skinned, boned and cut into chunks

300 ml/½ pint Fish Stock (see page 10)

12 fresh scallops, cleaned and halved

250 g/8 oz prawns, uncooked

salt and freshly ground black pepper

a few coriander leaves, torn, to garnish

heat the oil in a large, heavy-based saucepan and gently sauté the onion, garlic and the red and yellow peppers for about 10–15 minutes until they are tender.

add the tomatoes, ginger, chopped coriander, oregano, lime rind, chilli sauce and dried red chillies.

stir well to mix thoroughly and then simmer the mixture gently over low heat for 10 minutes.

add the monkfish and fish stock to the saucepan and bring to the boil. Reduce the heat and then simmer gently for 20 minutes.

stir in the scallops and prawns and cook gently for 2 more minutes until they are cooked.

season to taste with salt and pepper and serve the fish stew garnished with torn coriander leaves.

Serves: 6
Preparation time: *15 minutes*
Cooking time: *45 minutes*

clipboard: Scallops are usually sold opened and cleaned. To prepare them yourself, wash them in plenty of water. Open them by placing under a hot grill for 2–3 minutes, then insert a knife between the scallop and the half-shell to which it clings, and free the scallop. Remove the fringe area, and black intestinal thread. Retain only the white cushion and coral, and wash thoroughly.

River Trout

sautéed with almonds

A classic French recipe, this is an elegant combination. The hot, nut-flavoured butter sauce contrasts with the delicate taste and texture of the fish. For the best results, use the freshest trout available.

4 fresh trout, about 250 g/8 oz each, scaled and cleaned
200 ml/⅓ pint milk
1 tablespoon plain flour
1 tablespoon oil
150 g/5 oz butter
125 g/4 oz flaked almonds
salt and freshly ground black pepper

To garnish
lemon quarters
2 tablespoons finely chopped parsley

rinse the trout under running cold water. Pat dry with absorbent kitchen paper. Put the milk in one dish and the flour in another. Dip each trout into the milk and then coat with flour. Shake gently to remove any excess flour.

heat the oil and 125 g/4 oz of the butter in a large, heavy-bottomed frying pan. Add the trout and cook gently for about 5 minutes on each side until cooked and golden brown. Take care that the butter does not burn. Remove and place on a warmed serving dish. Sprinkle with salt and pepper and keep the trout warm.

wash out the frying pan and dry it thoroughly. Add the remaining butter and heat gently until the butter starts to foam.

add the almonds and cook over moderate heat for about 2 minutes, stirring constantly, until golden all over. Sprinkle the almonds and the butter in the pan over the trout and serve immediately, garnished with lemon quarters and sprinkled with parsley.

Serves: 4
Preparation time: *10 minutes*
Cooking time: *12 minutes*

Baked Sea Bream
with tarragon and lemon

Although there are so many delicious kinds of fish to sample from the fishmongers, most people remain faithful to their old favourites. The flavour of sea bream will be a delightful surprise if you have never tasted it before.

1 x 1–1.25 kg/2–2½ lb sea bream, cleaned and scaled
1 onion, sliced
25 g/1 oz butter
3 small tomatoes, halved
2 tablespoons Fish Stock (see page 10)
100 ml/3½ fl oz water
juice of 1 lemon
1 tablespoon fresh white breadcrumbs
1 tablespoon chopped tarragon
3 tablespoons olive oil

To garnish
1 lemon, halved
tarragon sprigs

place the fish in an ovenproof dish.

fry the onion gently in the butter over low heat for about 15 minutes or until soft and golden brown.

arrange the fried onion and halved tomatoes around the fish and then cover with the fish stock, water and lemon juice.

sprinkle the breadcrumbs, chopped tarragon and olive oil over the dish and then bake in a preheated oven, 180°C/350°F/Gas Mark 4, for 40–45 minutes, basting occasionally. Serve garnished with lemon and tarragon.

Serves: 6
Preparation time: *25 minutes*
Cooking time: *40–45 minutes*
Oven temperature: *180°C/350°F/Gas Mark 4*

clipboard: There are various kinds of sea bream available. This recipe uses the gilt-headed bream or *daurade,* which is its French name. Ask your fishmonger if you are unsure. Sea bream is delicious and comparatively inexpensive.

Fresh Tuna *baked with tomatoes, peppers and garlic*

1 kg/2 lb fresh tuna steaks, 2 cm/¾ inch thick

plain flour for dusting steaks

6 tablespoons olive oil

1 red pepper

1 green pepper

2 onions, sliced

2 large tomatoes, quartered

1 garlic clove, crushed

1 *bouquet garni*

200 ml/7 fl oz dry white wine

salt and freshly ground black pepper

2 tablespoons finely chopped basil to garnish

dust the tuna steaks with seasoned plain flour, then fry them gently in half of the olive oil over low heat, turning once to cook both sides. Remove from the pan and transfer them to an ovenproof dish.

place the red and green peppers under a hot grill in the meantime, turning occasionally until they are charred and blistered all over. Allow them to cool and then skin and slice the peppers, discarding the seeds.

fry the onions gently in the remaining olive oil until soft and golden brown. Add the peppers, tomatoes, garlic and *bouquet garni*.

season to taste and then simmer gently for 20 minutes. Add the wine and bring to the boil. Remove from the heat.

cover the tuna steaks with the sauce and then bake in a preheated oven, 200°C/400°F/Gas Mark 6, for 20 minutes.

reduce the oven temperature to 160°C/325°F/Gas Mark 3, cover the dish and cook the tuna for a further 30 minutes. Serve sprinkled with chopped basil.

Serves: 4–6
Preparation time: *30 minutes*
Cooking time: *50 minutes*
Oven temperature: *200°C/400°F/Gas Mark 6,*
then *160°C/325°F/Gas Mark 3*

Grey Mullet
with red wine and garlic

The flesh of grey mullet has a lovely flavour, and it is a fish that is worth buying when you see it at the fishmonger. Braised in red wine, it is scrumptious.

4 medium grey mullet or whiting, filleted
flour, for coating
75 ml/3 fl oz olive oil
3 tablespoons capers

Red wine sauce
2 tablespoons olive oil
2 onions, chopped
3 garlic cloves, crushed
2 tablespoons flour
500 ml/17 fl oz red wine
250 g/8 oz tomatoes, skinned (see page 20) and roughly chopped
2 tablespoons tomato purée
1 *bouquet garni*
salt and freshly ground black pepper

To garnish
2 tablespoons chopped parsley

make the sauce: heat the olive oil in a large saucepan and sauté the onions and garlic until soft and golden. Stir in the flour and cook gently for 1 minute, then add the red wine, stirring well. Bring to the boil.

add the tomatoes to the pan with the tomato purée, *bouquet garni* and seasoning, and then cook briskly, uncovered, for about 30 minutes or until the sauce is thick and reduced.

dust the fish fillets with flour in the meantime. Heat the olive oil in a large frying pan and cook the fish for 3–4 minutes each side, until they are cooked and golden. Remove from the pan, drain and keep warm.

pass the sauce through a sieve, or purée in a food processor or blender. Return to the pan and add the fish fillets. Heat through gently for 5–10 minutes. Add the capers and serve sprinkled with chopped parsley.

Serves: 4
Preparation time: *15 minutes*
Cooking time: *50–55 minutes*

Baked Monkfish
with green pepper sauce

1.25 kg/2½ lb monkfish tail,
skinned and filleted
1 teaspoon dried thyme
2 garlic cloves, cut into thin slivers
juice of ½ lemon
200 ml/7 fl oz dry white vermouth
salt and freshly ground black pepper
2 tablespoons chopped parsley, to garnish

Pepper sauce
3 tablespoons olive oil
2 green peppers, deseeded and chopped
2 onions, finely chopped
3 courgettes, chopped
salt and freshly ground black pepper

season the monkfish fillets with salt and pepper and sprinkle one of them with thyme. Make small incisions in the flesh with a sharp knife and carefully insert the slivers of garlic.

sprinkle with lemon juice and place the other fillet on top of the garlic-studded fillet. Secure with string. Place in an oiled ovenproof dish and add the vermouth. Cover with kitchen foil and bake in a preheated oven, 190°C/375°F/Gas Mark 5, for 30 minutes. Remove the fish and keep warm, reserving the cooking liquid.

make the sauce meanwhile: heat the olive oil in a heavy pan and fry the peppers for about 5 minutes, until softened. Add the onions, courgettes and seasoning and cook very gently, stirring occasionally, for 15 minutes.

add the reserved cooking liquid from the fish to the sauce and boil up for a few minutes, stirring well. Pour the sauce into a baking dish and place the fish on top. Return the baking dish to the oven for 15 minutes, or until the fish is cooked. Remove the string and serve hot, sprinkled with chopped parsley.

Serves: 4–6
Preparation time: *15 minutes*
Cooking time: *45 minutes*
Oven temperature: *190°C/375°F/Gas Mark 5*

clipboard: Monkfish (or anglerfish) has a superb flavour and texture, somewhat similar to that of lobster. It has become very popular and is now widely available at fishmongers and from the fresh fish counters at large supermarkets. It is quite expensive but well worth the money.

Seafood Brochettes *marinated in fresh lime juice*

juice of 2 limes
2 tablespoons olive oil
2 garlic cloves, crushed
500 g/1 lb mixed seafood – e.g. uncooked prawns,
fresh tuna, scallops
50 g/2 oz butter, softened
2 hot chillies, chopped (preferably jalapeño)
salt and freshly ground black pepper
few coriander leaves, torn, to garnish

To serve
plain boiled rice

make the marinade: put the squeezed juice of 2 limes with the olive oil and garlic in a large bowl. Mix thoroughly to blend and add some salt and pepper. Put the prepared seafood in the marinade (cut the scallops in half if they are very large) and stir gently until completely coated. Cover and refrigerate for at least 1 hour.

remove the seafood from the marinade and thread alternately on to wooden or metal skewers. Place them on the rack of a grill pan and brush with the remaining marinade. Grill, turning occasionally. until cooked and tender, about 5 minutes. Baste with more marinade if necessary.

make the chilli butter: blend the softened butter with the chopped chillies until they are thoroughly mixed. Arrange the seafood brochettes on 4 serving plates on a bed of rice and put a pat of chilli butter on top of each one. Scatter with torn coriander leaves.

Serves: 4
Preparation time: *20 minutes, plus 1 hour marinating*
Cooking time: *5 minutes*

clipboard: Hot chillies are the most fiery variety of pepper. The intensity of their heat increases as the chilli pepper matures, and can range from mild to scorching hot. Jalapeño chillies come from the Veracruz region of eastern Mexico.

Garlic Prawns
with chillies and limes

4 king prawns, uncooked
6 garlic cloves, peeled
2 red chillies, deseeded and chopped
3 tablespoons olive oil
50 g/2 oz butter
juice of 2 limes
½ teaspoon sea salt
½ teaspoon whole black peppercorns
3 tablespoons chopped coriander, to garnish

To serve
lime wedges
1 avocado, sliced

split the prawns carefully down the middle towards the tail end, without completely separating them. They should look rather similar to butterflies. Remove the dark vein running along the back of each prawn.

crush the garlic cloves with the sea salt, peppercorns and the chopped chillies using a pestle and mortar until you have a thick aromatic paste.

coat the prepared prawns with this garlic mixture and place them in a bowl. Scrape out any remaining garlic paste and spread over the prawns. Cover the bowl and leave in a cool place to marinate for at least 1 hour.

heat the olive oil and butter in a large, heavy-based frying pan and add the prawns and garlic paste. Quickly sauté them over medium heat for 2–3 minutes until they turn pink.

remove from the pan and keep warm. Add the lime juice to the pan and stir into the pan juices.

boil vigorously for a couple of minutes, then pour over the prawns. Garnish with coriander and serve with lime wedges, and avocado slices.

Serves: 4–6
Preparation time: *15 minutes, plus 1 hour marinating*
Cooking time: *5 minutes*

Grilled Seafood Shells
with garlic and mushrooms

600 ml/1 pint mussels, washed and scrubbed

175 g/6 oz queen scallops, cleaned and prepared

50 g/2 oz butter

1 tablespoon onion, finely chopped

1 garlic clove, crushed

50 g/2 oz button mushrooms, sliced

50 g/2 oz fresh white breadcrumbs

150 ml/¼ pint dry white wine

1 tablespoon lemon juice

1 tablespoon chopped parsley

salt and freshly ground black pepper

place the washed and scrubbed mussels in an ovenproof dish with a little water. Put in a preheated oven, 180 C°/350° F/Gas Mark 4, until they open. Remove the mussels from the shells, and separate the white and coral parts of the scallops.

melt half of the butter in a frying pan and sauté the onion, garlic and mushrooms until they are lightly coloured. Mix in the mussels and scallops and heat through gently.

butter 4 deep scallop shells and sprinkle in half of the breadcrumbs. Divide the seafood mixture between the shells. Boil 4 tablespoons of water with the wine and lemon juice until reduced and spoon over the shells.

combine the remaining breadcrumbs with the chopped parsley and seasoning and scatter over the shells. Melt the remaining butter and pour over the top. Place the shells on a baking tray and bake in a preheated oven, 180°C/350°F/Gas Mark 4, for 15 minutes until golden brown.

Serves: 4
Preparation time: *30 minutes*
Cooking time: *15 minutes*
Oven temperature:*180°C/350°F/Gas Mark 4*

Moules Marinière

mussels in wine and garlic

The all-time classic recipe for mussels, this has lots of delicious, fragrant sauce with a wonderful, aromatic flavour. Mop it up with plenty of French bread.

60 g/2½ oz butter

4 shallots, finely chopped

1 garlic clove, crushed

350 ml/12 fl oz dry white wine

1 *bouquet garni*

2 litres/3½ pints fresh mussels, washed and scrubbed

2 tablespoons chopped parsley

salt and freshly ground black pepper

French bread, to serve

melt the butter in a large saucepan, stir in the shallots and garlic and fry gently until soft. Stir in the wine, add the *bouquet garni* and bring to the boil. Boil for 2 minutes, add a pinch of salt and some black pepper to taste, and then add the mussels.

cover the pan and cook over high heat, shaking vigorously from time to time, until the mussel shells open. Remove from the pan with a slotted spoon and set aside. Discard any mussels that do not open.

boil the liquid rapidly until reduced by half, then return the mussels to the pan and heat through for 1 minute, shaking the pan constantly.

sprinkle with the parsley and shake the pan again. Pile the mussels up in a deep warmed serving dish or in individual dishes and pour the liquid over the top. Serve immediately with crusty French bread.

Serves: 4–6

Preparation time: *10–15 minutes*

Cooking time: *20 minutes*

Baked Scallops
with butter and breadcrumbs

This is the simplest method of cooking scallops, and relies completely on the freshness and purity of the fish. Use only the finest scallops for this recipe.

8–10 scallops with their shells, washed and prepared
125 g/4 oz butter
4 tablespoons fresh breadcrumbs
salt and freshly ground black pepper
2 tablespoons chopped parsley, to garnish

reserve the rounded part of 4 shells and chop the white flesh of the scallops coarsely, leaving the orange coral whole.

divide the chopped scallops and coral evenly between the 4 shells and season to taste. Dot the scallops with 50 g/2 oz butter.

sprinkle the fresh breadcrumbs equally between the shells and use the remaining butter to dot over the tops.

cook in the middle of a preheated oven, 180°C/350°F/Gas Mark 4, for about 30 minutes, or until the top is crisp and bubbly and the scallops are thoroughly cooked.

serve immediately, sprinkled with the fresh parsley.

Serves: 4
Preparation time: *30 minutes*
Cooking time: *30 minutes*
Oven temperature: *180°C/350°F/Gas Mark 4*

clipboard: The meat of the great scallop, with its pinkish-orange coral, is quite delectable. The smaller scallop is called the queen, and has tender, tasty meat. Both shells of the queen are rounded, while the great scallop has one flat half shell, and one rounded.

Poultry and
Game

Roast Chicken

with bread sauce and gravy

1 x 1.5–2 kg/3–4 lb oven-ready chicken with giblets
1 lemon
1 *bouquet garni*
4 tablespoons olive oil
salt and freshly ground black pepper

Bread sauce
600 ml/1 pint milk
1 small onion, grated
pinch of ground cloves
pinch of ground bay leaves
75 g/3 oz fresh white breadcrumbs
25 g/1oz butter
ground nutmeg
salt

Gravy
2 tablespoons plain flour
300 ml/½ pint Chicken Stock (see page 10), or wine
salt and freshly ground black pepper

remove the giblets from the chicken and reserve for the gravy stock.

put the lemon and the *bouquet garni* inside the chicken cavity and truss the chicken securely.

place the chicken in an oiled roasting tin, pour over the olive oil, and sprinkle with salt and pepper to taste.

roast in a preheated, oven, 180°C /350°F/Gas Mark 4, for 1½–1¾ hours or until the chicken is tender.

prepare the bread sauce 15 minutes before the chicken is cooked. Pour the milk into a pan and add the onion, cloves and bay leaves.

heat until the milk has almost reached boiling point. Stir in the breadcrumbs and butter. Remove from the heat and leave for 5 minutes. Add nutmeg and salt to taste.

make the gravy. Remove the chicken from the oven, and place on a serving dish in a warm place. Pour off all but 2 tablespoons of fat from the pan, leaving the residue. Add the flour to the pan, and stir over low heat until it is bubbling and golden. Gradually stir in the chicken stock or wine. Add salt and pepper to taste.

serve the chicken accompanied by the bread sauce and gravy.

Serves 6
Preparation time: *30 minutes*
Cooking time: *1½–1¾ hours*
Oven temperature: *180°C/350°F/Gas Mark 4*

Tequila Chicken
in pine-nut sauce

The ginger nuts in this unusual Mexican recipe thicken the sauce as well as adding extra flavour.

4 tablespoons sunflower or corn oil

4 chicken portions, preferably leg joints, skinned

2 garlic cloves, chopped

4 medium tomatoes, skinned (see page 20) and chopped

300 ml/½ pint Chicken Stock (see page 10)

few drops Tabasco sauce or a pinch of chilli powder

2 ginger nut biscuits

50 g/2 oz seedless raisins

2 tablespoons tequila or sherry

3 tablespoons pine nuts

salt and freshly ground black pepper

heat 2 tablespoons of the oil in a heavy bottomed frying pan and add the chicken. Cook steadily for 10 minutes, turning over once or twice. Remove from the pan with a perforated spoon. Heat the rest of the oil and add the garlic and tomatoes.

cook for a few minutes. Meanwhile, blend the chicken stock with the Tabasco sauce or chilli powder and pour over the ginger nut biscuits. When these are slightly softened, mash them with the liquid, or sieve, or blend in a liquidizer.

pour this mixture into the pan and stir to blend with the garlic and tomatoes. Add the chicken joints and raisins.

cover the pan and cook for about 10 minutes or until the chicken is tender. Finally, add the tequila or sherry, the pine nuts and any seasoning required. Heat for 2 minutes, then serve.

Serves 4
Preparation time: *30 minutes*
Cooking time: *45 minutes*

clipboard: Pine nuts are now widely available in large supermarkets and give a mild, creamy flavour to foods. Though they are used in many parts of the world, they are most familiar in Italian food – especially as a major ingredient in Pesto sauce.

Turkey and Orange Stir-Fry
with mixed vegetables

Marinade
1 tablespoon soy sauce
2 tablespoons orange juice

Stir-fry
350 g/12 oz turkey breast fillets, skinned
and cut into pieces 4 cm/1½ inch wide and thick
grated rind and juice of 2 oranges
1 tablespoon cornflour
1 tablespoon sunflower oil
1 teaspoon sesame seed oil
½ red pepper, deseeded and cut into neat strips
½ green pepper, deseeded and cut into neat strips
3 celery sticks, diced
125 g/4 oz carrots, peeled and cut
into matchstick slices
salt and freshly ground black pepper

To serve
plain boiled rice

make the marinade: mix the soy sauce and orange juice together. Place the turkey pieces in this and leave for 30 minutes.

measure the orange juice and add sufficient water to give 150 ml/ ¼ pint. Blend the cornflour with this and add a little salt and pepper. Lift the turkey from the marinade and drain well. Save the marinade.

heat the two oils in a wok or heavy frying pan. Add the turkey pieces and stir-fry for 4–5 minutes, then add the orange rind, peppers, celery and carrots. Continue stir-frying for a further 3 minutes.

pour in the cornflour and orange juice mixture, together with any marinade that may be left. Stir as the liquid comes to the boil and thickens slightly.

serve with plain boiled rice.

Serves 4
Preparation time: *25–30 minutes, plus 30 minutes marinating*
Cooking time: *9–10 minutes*

clipboard: Turkey has become very popular as a stir-fry ingredient, as it is tasty and has a good texture. It is now widely available in supermarkets ready-diced for cooking.

Coq au Vin

chicken in red wine

This is one of those recipes that immediately conjures up the essence of French cooking. The classic blend of long-simmered herbs, meat and wine is quite unforgettable.

2 tablespoons oil
50 g/2 oz butter
1 x 2.5 kg/5 lb chicken, cut into 12 serving pieces
24 small pickling onions, peeled
125 g/4 oz smoked bacon, diced
1 tablespoon plain flour
1 bottle good red wine, e.g. Burgundy
1 *bouquet garni*
2 garlic cloves, unpeeled
pinch of sugar
¼ teaspoon freshly grated nutmeg
24 button mushrooms
1 tablespoon brandy
3–4 slices French bread
oil for frying
salt and freshly ground black pepper
a few rosemary sprigs, to garnish
2 tablespoons chopped parsley, to serve

heat the oil and butter in a large flameproof casserole and add the chicken pieces. Fry gently over low heat until golden on all sides, turning occasionally. Remove with a slotted spoon and keep warm. Pour off a little of the fat from the casserole, then add the onions and bacon. Sauté until lightly coloured, then sprinkle in the flour and stir well.

pour in the wine and bring to the boil, stirring. Add the *bouquet garni*, garlic cloves, sugar and nutmeg, and salt and pepper to taste. Return the chicken to the casserole, lower the heat, cover and simmer for 15 minutes.

add the mushrooms and continue cooking gently for a further 45 minutes, or until the chicken is cooked and tender. Remove the chicken with a slotted spoon and arrange the pieces on a warm serving platter. Keep hot. Pour the brandy into the sauce and boil, uncovered, for 5 minutes until thick and reduced. Remove the *bouquet garni* and garlic.

remove the crusts from the bread and cut into pieces. Fry in oil until crisp and golden on both sides. Remove and pat with absorbent kitchen paper. Pour the sauce over the chicken and serve with the bread croûtes. Garnish with the rosemary and serve sprinkled with chopped parsley.

Serves 6–8
Preparation time: *15–20 minutes*
Cooking time: *1½ hours*

Basque-style Chicken *with garlic, ham, tomatoes and peppers*

4 tablespoons olive oil

175 g/6 oz smoked ham or streaky bacon, diced

4 large chicken portions

4 onions, sliced

3 garlic cloves, crushed

2 green peppers, deseeded and diced

¼ teaspoon dried marjoram

425 g/14 oz tomatoes, skinned (see page 20) and chopped *or* 1 x 425 g/14 oz can of tomatoes

150–300 ml/¼–½ pint Chicken Stock (see page 10)

salt and freshly ground black pepper

2 tablespoons chopped parsley, to garnish

heat the olive oil in a sauté pan or deep frying pan. Add the diced ham or bacon and sauté gently, stirring occasionally, until lightly browned. Remove the ham from the pan with a slotted spoon and keep warm.

add the chicken portions to the pan and cook, turning occasionally, until they are uniformly brown. Remove with a slotted spoon and keep warm. Add the onions and garlic and cook gently until soft and golden. Add the peppers and marjoram, cover and cook gently for 10 minutes.

add the tomatoes and some stock (300 ml/½ pint if you are using fresh tomatoes, or 150 ml/¼ pint if you are using canned tomatoes in juice). Season to taste with salt and pepper. Return the chicken and ham to the pan, cover and cook gently for 40–45 minutes, or until the chicken is cooked and tender.

remove the chicken and transfer to a serving dish. Boil the sauce gently to reduce if necessary, until it is thick enough to coat the back of a spoon. Adjust the seasoning and pour over the chicken. Sprinkle with chopped parsley and serve.

Serves 4
Preparation time: *20 minutes*
Cooking time: *1 hour*

Chicken and Olives
with fresh herbs and garlic

175 g/6 oz black olives, pitted and chopped
1 tablespoon chopped parsley
1 tablespoon chopped chervil
1 tablespoon chopped tarragon
1 tablespoon chopped watercress
3 garlic cloves, chopped
150 g/5 oz butter, melted
4 chicken portions
3 tablespoons olive oil
1 *bouquet garni*
salt and freshly ground black pepper

mix half of the black olives with all the fresh herbs, the watercress, garlic and melted butter. Season with salt and pepper.

rub the prepared herb, olive and butter mixture all over the chicken portions, and then transfer them to a large ovenproof dish.

prick the skin of the chicken all over with a sharp knife, and then sprinkle with the olive oil. Add the *bouquet garni* to the dish.

roast the chicken in a preheated oven, 200°C/400°F/Gas Mark 6, for 35–40 minutes.

remove the *bouquet garni* and serve the chicken garnished with the remaining olives.

Serves 4
Preparation time: *10 minutes*
Cooking time: *35–45 minutes*
Oven temperature: *200°C/400°F/Gas Mark 6*

Provençal Chicken
with fragrant herbs

1 x 1.5–2 kg/3–4 lb chicken
juice of 1 lemon
3 tablespoons olive oil
25 g/1 oz butter, melted
pinch of Provençal herbs
1 lemon, peeled and sliced
salt and freshly ground black pepper
lemon slices, to garnish

wash and dry the chicken, place in a roasting tin, and brush it all over with the lemon juice.

mix 2 tablespoons of olive oil with the butter, salt, pepper and herbs. Coat the chicken with this sauce.

place the lemon slices inside the chicken, then roast in a preheated oven, 180°C /350°F/Gas Mark 4, for 1½–1¾ hours.

sprinkle the chicken with the remaining olive oil just before carving.

serve the chicken garnished with lemon slices and accompanied by plain boiled rice or vegetables.

Serves 4
Preparation time: *10 minutes*
Cooking time: *1½–1¾ hours*
Oven temperature: *180°C /350°F/Gas Mark 4*

clipboard: the fragrant wild herbs of Provence are often mixed and dried and then sold in pots as *herbes de Provence*. The ones frequently used are bay, fennel, marjoram, oregano, rosemary and thyme. Use them to flavour meat and vegetable stews, to sprinkle over grilled or barbecued fish, meat and poultry, and to enhance vegetables, soups and gratins.

Burgundy Pheasants

2 plump young pheasants with giblets
small sprig of thyme or pinch dried thyme
50 g/2 oz butter
300 ml/½ pint red Burgundy wine
1 tablespoon arrowroot or cornflour
2 tablespoons redcurrant jelly
2 tablespoons cocktail onions
2 tablespoons stuffed green olives (optional)
salt and freshly ground black pepper

To garnish
redcurrants
parsley sprigs

put the pheasant giblets into a pan with water to cover, add a little salt and pepper and thyme. Cover the pan and simmer for 45 minutes. Strain the liquid and boil briskly until reduced to 300 ml/½ pint stock. If you have no giblets to make stock, use Chicken Stock (see page 10).

put 25 g/1 oz of the butter inside the birds and spread the remainder over the skin. Put them into a roasting tin, and cover lightly with kitchen foil to keep from drying out. Place in a preheated oven, 200°C/400°F/Gas Mark 6, and roast for 40 minutes. Bring the roasting tin out of the oven about 10 minutes before the birds are cooked. Lift them on to a dish and pour out all the fat, straining 1 tablespoon into a pan for the sauce. Replace the birds and pour 3 tablespoons of the wine over them. Return to the oven while you make the sauce.

make the sauce: blend the arrowroot or cornflour with the remaining wine, and add to the fat in the pan with the redcurrant jelly and giblet stock. Stir as the sauce comes to the boil, thickens slightly and the jelly dissolves. Lift the pheasants on to a heated dish. Strain the juices from the roasting tin into the sauce. Boil for a few minutes, then add the well-drained onions and olives, if using, and any extra seasoning required. Heat for 2–3 minutes.

Pour the sauce over the pheasants, and garnish with redcurrants and sprigs of parsley. Serve with accompaniments such as bacon rolls, game chips, fried crumbs, small sausages etc.

Serves 4–6
Preparation time: *20 minutes*
Cooking time: *40 minutes*
Oven temperature: *200°C/400°F/Gas Mark 6*

Duck with Oranges

25 g/1 oz butter
3 tablespoons olive oil
1 x 2 kg/4 lb duck, trussed with thread or string
4 garlic cloves, crushed
125 g/4 oz raw country ham, cut into thin strips
600 ml/1 pint dry white wine
200 ml/7 fl oz Chicken Stock (see page 10)
1 *bouquet garni*
pared rind, and juice of 2 oranges
1 tablespoon wine vinegar
salt and freshly ground black pepper
2 oranges, cut into thin rings, to garnish

Beurre manié
1 tablespoon flour
25 g/1 oz butter, softened

heat the butter and oil in a deep flameproof casserole and add the duck. Fry over medium heat, turning the duck as necessary, until it is golden brown all over.

add the garlic and strips of ham to the casserole and fry for 1–2 minutes. Pour in the white wine and stock, bring to the boil and then simmer for a few minutes until slightly reduced. Add the *bouquet garni*, salt and pepper and orange juice, and then cover the casserole. Reduce the heat and simmer gently for 1½ hours, or until the duck is cooked. Baste occasionally during cooking.

cut the pared orange rind into fine strips with a sharp knife, and plunge them into a small pan of boiling water. Blanch for 5 minutes, then remove and drain. Dry thoroughly on absorbent kitchen paper and set aside.

make the *beurre manié:* blend the flour and butter thoroughly to make a smooth paste. Remove the duck from the casserole, cut into serving pieces and keep warm. Boil the cooking liquid for about 10 minutes, until reduced. Add the vinegar, strips of orange rind and little pieces of *beurre manié*, a few at a time, stirring constantly, until the sauce thickens.

carve and serve with the orange sauce, garnished with orange rings.

Serves 6
Preparation time: *20 minutes*
Cooking time: about *1¾–2 hours*

Game Pie

This is a traditional game pie from East Anglia, which is world famous for its large shoots and excellent game. This pie tastes just as good eaten cold.

25 g/1 oz butter
1 large onion, finely chopped
2 partridges or 1 other small game bird
or 1 pheasant, cleaned and jointed
250 g/8 oz lean steak, cut into 2.5 cm/1 inch pieces
2 rashers bacon, rinded and cut into
1 cm/½ inch strips
125 g/4 oz mushrooms
1 thyme sprig
1 bay leaf
600 ml/1 pint Beef Stock (see page 10)
300 g/10 oz shortcrust or flaky pastry
1 egg, beaten
salt and freshly ground black pepper

melt the butter in a frying pan, add the onion and cook until soft. Add the game joints and brown on all sides. Remove from the pan and reserve. Add the steak and brown lightly.

spread the steak on the bottom of a large pie dish and arrange the game joints on top. Sprinkle the onion, bacon, mushrooms and herbs on top. Season to taste and just cover with stock. Cover with kitchen foil and cook in a preheated oven, 150°C/300°F/Gas Mark 2, for about 1½–2 hours until the meat is tender.

remove the dish from the oven and allow to cool. Increase the oven temperature to 200°C/400°F/Gas Mark 6. Add a little more stock to bring the liquid 1 cm/½ inch from the top of the meat.

roll out the pastry and cut out a lid to fit the dish. Cut a strip 2.5 cm/1 inch wide and lay it around the rim of the dish. Moisten with water, then lay on the pastry lid, pressing it down firmly. Knock back the edges and mark with a knife in ridges. Brush with beaten egg. Roll out the trimmings and use to make leaves or other decorations. Place on the lid and brush with egg again. Return to the oven and bake for 20 minutes.

reduce the oven heat to 150°C/300°F/ Gas Mark 2, place the pie on a lower shelf in the oven and bake for a further 15–20 minutes.

Serves 6
Preparation time: *30 minutes, plus cooling*
Cooking time: *2¼–2¼ hours*
Oven temperature: *150°C/300°F/Gas Mark 2, then 200°C/400°F/Gas Mark 6, then 150°C/300°F/Gas Mark 2*

Pasta and Rice

Meat-filled Cannelloni

1–2 tablespoons olive oil
375 g/12 oz lean stewing veal, finely diced
1 onion, sliced
1 carrot, sliced
150 ml/5 fl oz dry white wine
300 ml/½ pint Chicken Stock (see page 10)
125 g/4 oz chicken, cooked
125 g/4 oz spinach, cooked and chopped
2–3 tablespoons single cream
12 tubes ready-to-cook cannelloni
2 x quantity Tomato Sauce (see page 8)
40 g/1½ oz Parmesan cheese, grated
salt and freshly ground black pepper

butter an oven-to-table dish and set aside. Heat the oil in a pan and fry the veal until it is golden brown. Remove from the pan, add the vegetables and cook until lightly coloured. Return the veal to the pan with the wine and stock. Season lightly and simmer gently for 40–45 minutes until the meat is tender.

remove the meat and vegetables from the pan and mince or chop finely in a food processor with the chicken. Stir in the chopped spinach. Boil the stock until it has reduced to about 2 tablespoons and stir it into the meat and spinach mixture with sufficient cream to soften the mixture.

pipe or spoon the filling into the cannelloni tubes. Place the filled cannelloni in the oven-to-table dish and pour the tomato sauce over. Bake in a preheated oven, 180°C/350°F/Gas Mark 4, for 40–45 minutes.

sprinkle a little Parmesan over the top 5–10 minutes before the end of the cooking time and serve the rest separately.

Serves 4
Preparation time: *20–30 minutes*
Cooking time: *1–1½ hours*
Oven temperature: *180°C/350°F/Gas Mark 4*

clipboard: To improve the texture of ready-to-cook cannelloni tubes, place them one by one into a dish of boiling water for 1 minute, then drain them well before using. This applies to all ready-to-cook pasta. The simplest way to fill cannelloni tubes is to put the filling mixture into a piping bag, without the nozzle, and squeeze it gently into the tubes.

Spinach Lasagne

baked with cheese sauce

500–750g/1–1½ lb fresh spinach, cleaned and
chopped or 375g/12 oz frozen leaf spinach
1½ tablespoons olive oil
2 onions, finely chopped
2 garlic cloves, finely chopped
10 sheets of ready-to-cook lasagne
salt and freshly ground black pepper

Cheese sauce

50 g/2 oz butter or margarine
50 g/2 oz flour
750 ml/1¼ pints milk
1–2 eggs (optional)
175 g/6 oz Gruyère or Cheddar cheese, grated
2 or 3 tablespoons Parmesan cheese, grated
1 teaspoon English mustard, made up
salt and freshly ground black pepper

cook the fresh spinach in the water left on the leaves after washing; add salt and pepper to taste. Strain thoroughly, then chop finely. Cook frozen spinach as instructed on the packet. Heat the oil, add the onions and garlic and cook until tender. Mix with the spinach.

make the cheese sauce: heat the butter or margarine in a saucepan, stir in the flour, then gradually add the milk. Bring to the boil, then stir or whisk into a smooth sauce.

beat the eggs well, if adding, then whisk into the hot, but not boiling sauce. Do not reheat. Grate the cheese and stir most of it into the sauce, with the mustard and salt and pepper.

place the layers of lasagne, spinach and sauce in an ovenproof dish, beginning with lasagne and ending with lasagne and a coating of sauce.

sprinkle the last of the Gruyère or Cheddar and the Parmesan over the top of the sauce and bake for 25–30 minutes in a preheated oven, 190°C/375°F/Gas Mark 5. Serve hot.

Serves 4
Preparation time: *40 minutes*
Cooking time: *25–30 minutes*
Oven temperature: *190°C/375°F/Gas Mark 5*

Tagliatelle Verde

with bacon, garlic and fennel

6 rashers unsmoked streaky bacon
2 tablespoons olive oil
2 fennel bulbs, finely chopped
2 garlic cloves, finely chopped
4 tablespoons freshly grated Parmesan cheese
300 ml/½ pint fromage frais
3 tablespoons finely chopped parsley
375 g/12 oz spinach tagliatelle (fresh or dried)
salt and freshly ground black pepper
fennel fronds, to garnish

grill the bacon until crisp. Drain on absorbent kitchen paper and set aside. Heat the oil in a pan and add the fennel and garlic.

cover the pan and cook gently over a low heat for 5 minutes until the fennel is just tender.

add the Parmesan, fromage frais and parsley, and season to taste. Simmer over a low heat for 1–2 minutes.

cook the pasta in boiling salted water until *al dente* or just firm to the bite. This will take about 3 minutes for fresh pasta and 10–15 minutes for dried. Drain and toss with the sauce. Transfer to a heated serving dish.

chop the bacon and sprinkle over the pasta. Garnish with fennel fronds and serve at once.

Serves 4–6
Preparation time: *15 minutes*
Cooking time: *15–30 minutes*

clipboard: Green tagliatelle (or tagliatelle verde) is made with spinach – hence the green colour. Spinach is used to make a wide range of green pasta, and looks brilliantly colourful.

Fettuccine *with chilli, prosciutto and tomato sauce*

4 tablespoons olive oil
1 onion, finely chopped
125 g/4 oz prosciutto, diced
2 garlic cloves, crushed
1 fresh chilli, deseeded and finely chopped
750 g/1½ lb tomatoes, skinned (see page 20)
and chopped
500 g/1 lb fettuccine or tagliatelle (fresh or dried)
salt and freshly ground black pepper
75 g/3 oz pecorino cheese, freshly grated, to serve

heat the oil in a pan, and gently fry the onion for 3 minutes. Add the prosciutto and cook for a further 2–3 minutes.

add the garlic, chilli and tomatoes, and season to taste with salt and pepper. Cook gently for 10 minutes until thickened.

cook the pasta in boiling salted water until *al dente* or just firm to the bite. This will take about 3 minutes for fresh pasta and 10–15 minutes for dried. Drain and toss with the sauce and grated pecorino.

transfer to a heated serving dish and serve immediately.

Serves 4–6
Preparation time: *15 minutes*
Cooking time: *20–35 minutes*

clipboard: Pecorino Romano is a hard, grating cheese not dissimilar to Parmesan. It has been made for two thousand years in southern Italy. The main ingredient is sheep's milk, and this gives the cheese a very distinctive salty, tangy taste. The name is taken from the word 'pecora' which means ewe. There are several kinds of pecorino, which is generally used like Parmesan.

Oils and Vinegars

Sunflower oil

Pistachio oil

Extra-virgin olive oil

Lemon oil

Corn oil

Walnut oil

Sesame oil

Grapeseed oil

Sesame oil
Sesame oil is extracted from sesame seeds and is used in Oriental cookery to flavour traditional dishes. It is rarely used for frying as it has a low smoking point.

Sunflower oil
High in polyunsaturated fatty acids, it is extracted from sunflower seeds and is used in all cooking methods. It has a light, bland flavour.

Corn oil
This is an extract of maize (corn). It is a light golden and delicately flavoured oil which can be used for frying, salad dressings, mayonnaise and baking. It is high in polyunsaturated fatty acids.

Grapeseed oil
A light, pale green oil extracted from grape seeds, it is used in all methods of cooking, including frying and baking. It imparts very little flavour to foods so is useful when it is essential not to mask the delicate flavours of fish or poultry.

Pistachio oil
A distinctive, fine-quality oil which is expensive to produce and therefore costly to buy, it is used in dressings for its strong nutty flavour.

Walnut oil
An expensive, fine-quality oil made from walnuts, and containing polyunsaturated fatty acids, it has a delicate nutty flavour and is used mainly for salad dressings.

Lemon oil
Lemon oil is used instead of lemon essence, or in light salad dressings. It should be kept in a dark, well-stoppered bottle to preserve flavour.

Extra-virgin olive oil
To be labelled extra virgin, olive oil must be from the first pressing of small, ripe olives and have an acidity of 0.2–1 per cent. Extra-virgin olive oil is expensive and is mostly used in dressings.

Olive oil
A golden green oil with a rich, fruity flavour, this is a blending of oils from second

Balsamic vinegar

Red wine vinegar

Sherry vinegar

Raspberry vinegar

Malt vinegar

White wine vinegar with rosemary

Olive oil

or subsequent pressing, which are then subjected to a process of refinement, with first pressed virgin oils. In Latin countries, olive oil is used for all cooking. It is a good source of mono-unsaturated fatty acids.

Balsamic vinegar

This is the most expensive vinegar available. It is aged in wooden casks for 10–30 years. The finest comes from Modena in northern Italy. It is slightly sweet and is used in dressings and sauces.

Red wine vinegar

This is produced in most of the wine-producing regions of the world and each has its own flavour, depending on the grapes in the region. Chianti vinegar, for example, is made from the light red wines of the Chianti region in Tuscany.

Darker red wine vinegars come from the grape skins being left in the juice.

Sherry vinegar

Rich, mellow sherry vinegar comes from Spain and is distilled in the same manner as sherry. The flavour is very strong, so it is used sparingly in dressings.

Malt vinegar

This is made from malted barley, and originates from northern Europe. It has a very acid flavour and is best used for pickling.

Raspberry vinegar

Raspberry vinegar is made by infusing the flavour of the fruit in white wine vinegar. The vinegar is reduced to burn off the acidity, leaving only the flavour. This is particularly good in salad dressings.

White wine vinegar with rosemary

Herb vinegars like white wine vinegar with rosemary are also made by infusion (see raspberry vinegar). They should be used in dressings where you would use the herb to complement the dish. Basil vinegar, for example, can be used in tomato salads. Tarragon vinegar is delicious with chicken and fish dishes.

Penne *with bacon, mushroom and tomato*

125 g/4 oz butter
175 g/6 oz lean bacon, diced
375 g/12 oz mushrooms, sliced
2 garlic cloves, sliced
½ fresh chilli, deseeded
500 g/1 lb tomatoes, skinned (see page 20) and chopped
few basil leaves, torn
500 g/1 lb penne or macaroni (fresh or dried)
125 g/4 oz Parmesan cheese, freshly grated
or 125 g/4 oz pecorino cheese, freshly grated
salt

melt half the butter in a frying pan, add the bacon and gently fry until lightly browned. Remove from the pan with a slotted spoon, and drain on absorbent kitchen paper.

fry the mushrooms in the butter remaining in the pan. Remove with a slotted spoon and set aside. Fry the garlic and the chilli in the same pan. When the garlic is golden brown, discard it, together with the chilli.

add the tomatoes to the pan with the basil. Season with salt and simmer for 20 minutes. Stir in the bacon and mushrooms, and simmer gently for a few minutes.

cook the pasta in boiling salted water until *al dente* or just firm to the bite. This will take about 3 minutes for fresh pasta and 10–15 minutes for dried pasta.

drain and transfer to a heated serving dish. Toss with the cheeses and the remaining butter. Pour the sauce over the top, toss gently and serve.

Serves 4–6
Preparation time: *15 minutes*
Cooking time: *35–45*

clipboard: Fresh chillies are easily available at supermarkets and grocers. The seeds are the hottest part. Wear rubber gloves to remove them. Slit the chilli lengthways down the centre, hold it under a cold tap, and rub off the seeds. When handling chillies, don't put your fingers near your eyes, as the pungent juices will irritate and sting them.

Tagliatelle

in smoked salmon and asparagus sauc

375 g/12 oz asparagus
375 g/12 oz tagliatelle or fettuccine (fresh or dried)
125 g/4 oz smoked salmon, cut into thin strips
300 ml/½ pint double cream
1 tablespoon chopped tarragon
salt and freshly ground black pepper
Parmesan shavings, to garnish

cut off the asparagus tips and blanch in boiling salted water for 5 minutes. Use the stems for soup or stock.

drain the tips under cold running water, and pat dry.

cook the pasta in boiling salted water until *al dente* or just firm to the bite. This will take about 3 minutes for fresh pasta and 10–15 minutes for dried pasta.

drain and return to the pan. Toss over a low heat with the asparagus, smoked salmon, cream, tarragon, and salt and pepper, until it is completely heated through.

transfer to a heated serving dish and garnish with wafer-thin shavings of Parmesan.

Serves 4
Preparation time: *10 minutes*
Cooking time: *10–25 minutes*

clipboard: For Smoked Salmon and Mushroom Sauce, use 375 g/12 oz mixed ceps, shiitake, oyster and chestnut mushrooms, instead of the asparagus. Cut into even–sized pieces and stir-fry in 2 tablespoons of olive oil for 5–7 minutes, before adding to the pasta.

Spaghetti
in pepper, aubergine and olive sauce

4 tablespoons olive oil
1 onion, finely chopped
1 x 425 g/14 oz can chopped tomatoes
2 tablespoon tomato purée
150 ml/¼ pint red wine
1 large aubergine, chopped
1 large red pepper, cored, deseeded and finely diced
1 large green pepper, cored, deseeded and finely diced
8 anchovy fillets, drained and chopped
1 garlic clove, crushed
500 g/1 lb spaghetti or linguine (fresh or dried)
75 g/3 oz black olives, pitted
salt and freshly ground black pepper

heat the oil in a pan, and gently fry the onion for 3 minutes.

add the tomatoes, tomato purée, red wine, aubergine, red and green peppers, anchovy fillets and garlic. Simmer gently for 20 minutes.

cook the pasta in boiling salted water until *al dente* or just firm to the bite. This will take about 3 minutes for fresh pasta and 10–15 minutes for dried pasta.

drain and toss with the sauce, adding the olives, and salt and pepper to taste. Serve immediately.

Serves 4–6
Preparation time: *10 minutes*
Cooking time: *23–35 minutes*

Spaghetti
with roasted peppers, coriander and chilli pesto

3 mixed red and yellow peppers
500 g/1 lb spaghetti or fettuccine (fresh or dried)
50 g/2 oz butter, diced

Coriander and chilli pesto
50 g/2 oz fresh coriander, roughly chopped
1 fresh chilli, deseeded and roughly chopped
2 garlic cloves, crushed
2 tablespoons pine nuts
finely grated rind of 1 lime
1 teaspoon salt
8 tablespoons olive oil
50 g/2 oz Parmesan cheese, freshly grated

roast the peppers in a preheated oven, 220°C/425°F/Gas Mark 7, until the skins blacken on all sides.

remove the skins and seeds, then chop the flesh into 1 cm/½ inch dice.

make the coriander and chilli pesto: put the coriander and chilli in a blender or food processor with the garlic, pine nuts, lime rind and salt.

purée until smooth, gradually adding the olive oil. Transfer to a bowl and mix with the Parmesan.

cook the pasta in boiling salted water until *al dente* or just firm to the bite. This will take about 3 minutes for fresh pasta and 10–15 minutes for dried pasta.

drain and toss with the peppers, sauce and butter. Serve immediately.

Serves 6
Preparation time: *20 minutes*
Cooking time: *20–30 minutes*
Oven temperature: *220°C/425°F/Gas Mark 7*

Kedgeree

This is one of the many Anglo-Indian dishes that came from the era of the British Raj. The name derives from the Hindu word khichri (a purée of of rice and lentils, or dhal). The addition of the smoked fish results in a luscious, creamy blend of flavours and textures.

125 g/4 oz long-grain rice
500 g/1 lb smoked haddock
2 eggs
50 g/2 oz butter or margarine
2–3 tablespoons milk or single cream
salt and freshly ground black pepper
chopped parsley, to garnish

cook the rice in boiling salted water for about 12 minutes, or according to the packet instructions, until each grain is dry and fluffy, then set aside.

poach the haddock in a little water for 10 minutes, drain and break the fish into large flakes. Meanwhile, hard-boil the eggs, shell, cut half an egg into wedges for a garnish and chop the rest.

heat the butter or margarine in a large pan, add the fish and the cooked rice and just enough milk or cream to moisten. Heat gently, stirring carefully, so the flakes of fish are not broken. Add the chopped eggs to the mixture and season to taste.

spoon on to a heated dish and top with the parsley and garnish with the egg wedges.

Serves 4
Preparation time: *10 minutes*
Cooking time: *30 minutes*

clipboard: While this is an excellent way of using left-over cooked smoked haddock or other fish, it is so good that it is worthwhile cooking the haddock specially. The fillet is better than a whole fish in this case.

Traditional Paella

Paella is so colourful, fragrant and full of flavour, it is not surprising that it is Spain's most popular dish! It is named after the pan in which it is cooked.

2 tablespoons olive oil

1 small chicken, cut into 8 portions

125 g/4 oz fat pork or bacon, diced

1 large Spanish onion, chopped

2–3 garlic cloves

500 g/1 lb tomatoes, skinned (see page 20) and chopped

1 red pepper cored, deseeded and sliced

250–300 g/8–10 oz arborio rice

600 ml/1 pint boiling water

¼ teaspoon saffron powder or strands

75 g/3 oz chorizo (spicy Spanish sausage), or any spiced sausage thinly sliced

12 mussels on half their shells

12 large prawns, shelled and cleaned

salt and freshly ground black pepper

heat the oil and fry the chicken and pork or bacon until golden and nearly tender. Remove from the pan, add the onion and garlic and cook for 5 minutes or until golden brown.

put in the tomatoes and cook for 2–3 minutes, then add the red pepper and rice.

continue to stir over a gentle heat for 1–2 minutes, mixing the rice with the onion mixture. Boil the water, add the saffron and pour over the rice. Season lightly.

cook steadily until the rice is almost tender. Stir from time to time and make sure that you check the amount of liquid regularly. If necessary, add more boiling water.

return the chicken and pork or bacon to the mixture and continue cooking until almost ready to serve.

add the sausage to the pan with the mussels and prawns and any extra seasoning required. Heat for 5–7 minutes.

serve straight from the paella pan.

Serves 4
Preparation time: *50 minutes*
Cooking time: *35–40 minutes*

Fragrant Rice
with vegetables and cashew nuts

This is a delightfully light and fresh way of cooking rice. It is excellent as part of an Oriental meal, or as a delicious vegetarian dish in its own right.

250 g/8 oz easy-cook long-grain rice

1 cinnamon stick

seeds of 4–6 cardamom pods

3–4 cloves

3 tablespoons vegetable oil

1 green pepper, cored, deseeded and finely chopped

1 onion, finely chopped

1 garlic clove, crushed

125 g/ 4 oz button mushrooms, thinly sliced

125 g/4 oz frozen peas

175 ml/6 fl oz vegetable stock, or water

2 carrots, peeled and grated

100 g/3½ oz cashew nuts

salt and freshly ground black pepper

cook the rice in boiling salted water according to packet instructions, with the cinnamon stick, cardamom seeds and cloves until each grain is dry and fluffy. Drain and set aside, removing the spices.

heat a wok until hot. Add the oil and heat over a moderate heat until hot. Add the green pepper, onion and garlic and stir-fry for 2–3 minutes or until softened slightly.

add the mushrooms and frozen peas, increase the heat to high and stir-fry for 3–4 minutes or until tender.

add the cooked rice and stock or water to the wok and toss to mix with the vegetables, then stir in the grated carrots and about three-quarters of the cashew nuts.

toss for a further minute. Add salt and pepper to taste and serve at once, sprinkled with the remaining cashew nuts.

Serves 4 as an accompaniment
Preparation time: *40 minutes*
Cooking time: *15–20 minutes*

Vegetables

Ratatouille
braised Mediterranean vegetables

Ratatouille is one of those dishes that instantly evokes the spirit of the south of France. The mix of flavours, colours and textures is utterly delicious.

4 tablespoons olive oil
3 onions, finely chopped
3 garlic cloves, finely chopped
750 g/1½ lb tomatoes, skinned (see page 20) and chopped
5 courgettes, sliced
2 large aubergines, sliced
salt and freshly ground black pepper
2 tablespoons chopped parsley

heat the oil and cook the onions and garlic gently for 5 minutes. Add the tomatoes and cook for a few minutes until the juice starts to flow.

add the courgettes and aubergines and stir them all together to mix well. Add a little salt and pepper.

cover the pan and simmer for about 30 minutes, or until the vegetables are softened.

taste and add extra seasoning if necessary, then stir in some of the chopped parsley. Serve with some more parsley sprinkled on the top.

Serves 6–8
Preparation time: *15–20 minutes*
Cooking time: *1 hour*

clipboard: Ratatouille is equally good eaten hot or cold. Make several batches of it in the summer months when there are plentiful supplies of the ingredients available. It freezes well for at least a year, and makes an excellent stand-by dish.

Vegetable Moussaka

50 g/2 oz margarine

3 tablespoons sunflower or corn oil

2 aubergines, thinly sliced

4 potatoes, peeled and thinly sliced

3 large onions, chopped

2 garlic cloves, chopped

3 large tomatoes, skinned (see page 20) and sliced

salt and freshly ground black pepper

Cheese sauce

50 g/2 oz margarine

40 g/1½ oz wholemeal flour

600 ml/1 pint milk

250 g/8 oz Cheddar cheese, grated

½-1 teaspoon mixed spice or grated nutmeg

1 teaspoon French mustard

salt and freshly ground black pepper

1 tablespoon chopped parsley, to garnish (optional)

heat half the margarine and oil in a pan, add the aubergines and potato slices and cook steadily for 10 minutes, turning over once or twice. Remove from the pan.

heat the rest of the margarine and oil, add the onions, garlic and tomatoes and cook for 10 minutes; make sure they do not brown. Mix half the aubergines and potatoes with the tomato mixture and season to taste. Keep the rest of the aubergines and potatoes to make the topping.

make the sauce: heat the margarine, add the flour and stir over the heat for 1–2 minutes, then gradually blend in the milk. Stir until a smooth sauce is formed. Remove from the heat, add approximately 175 g/6 oz of the cheese and season with salt, pepper, mixed spice or nutmeg and mustard.

spoon half of the mixed vegetables into a casserole, add half of the sauce and the remainder of the mixed vegetables. Top with a neat layer of aubergines and potatoes, then the rest of the sauce.

cover the casserole with a lid or foil; make sure this does not touch the sauce. Bake for 1¼ hours in a preheated oven, 160°C/325°F, Gas Mark 3. Remove the lid, add the remaining cheese, return to the oven, raising the heat slightly, and cook for a further 10 minutes, or until the cheese topping has melted. Garnish with chopped parsley, if liked.

Serves 4
Preparation time: *15 minutes*
Cooking time: *about 2 hours*
Oven temperature: *160°C/325°F/Gas Mark 3*

Stuffed Artichokes

4 globe artichokes, cleaned and trimmed

juice of ½ lemon

1 onion, thinly sliced

2 carrots, thinly sliced

1 bay leaf

250 ml/8 fl oz dry white wine

250 ml/8 fl oz water

1 tablespoon arrowroot

salt and freshly ground black pepper

Savoury stuffing

2 tablespoons olive oil

1 onion, finely chopped

2 garlic cloves, crushed

125 g/4 oz raw ham or streaky bacon, chopped

2 tablespoons chopped parsley

50 g/2 oz fresh breadcrumbs

salt and freshly ground black pepper

sprinkle the trimmed artichokes with lemon juice and set aside until you are ready to cook them. Put them in a pan of boiling salted water, simmer for 10–15 minutes and then drain upside-down. Remove the fibrous choke in the centre of each artichoke with a small spoon.

make the stuffing: heat the olive oil in a saucepan and fry the onion and garlic over low heat until soft and golden. Remove from the heat and add the ham or bacon, parsley and breadcrumbs. Stir well and season to taste.

fill the hollow centre of each prepared artichoke with the stuffing mixture. Put the onion and carrots in a flameproof casserole and place the artichokes on top. Add the bay leaf and pour over the wine and water, and add a little salt and pepper. Bring to the boil, then reduce the heat and simmer gently for 45 minutes.

remove the artichokes and keep warm. Strain the cooking liquid into a small saucepan and add the arrowroot which has been dissolved in 3 tablespoons of water. Heat gently, stirring all the time, until the sauce has a creamy consistency. Season to taste and serve hot with the artichokes.

Serves 4
Preparation time: *40 minutes*
Cooking time: *1–1¼ hours*

clipboard: Fresh artichokes have a wonderful flavour, and are easy to prepare for cooking. Remove the stalks and the leaves at the base of each artichoke. Cut off the ends of the leaves. Sprinkle with lemon juice to prevent them discolouring until they are used in the recipe.

Vegetables
in Cream Sauce

served on a bed of pasta

125 g/4 oz butter
1 onion, diced
1 carrot, diced
1 celery stalk, diced
125 g/4 oz peas, shelled
2 ripe tomatoes, skinned (see page 20) and chopped
1 large courgette, cut into 1 cm/½ inch cubes
125 g/4 oz thin asparagus stalks chopped
300 ml/½ pint double cream
500 g/1 lb fettuccine or tagliatelle (fresh or dried)
50 g/2 oz Parmesan cheese, freshly grated
2 tablespoons flat-leaf finely chopped parsley
salt and freshly ground black pepper

melt half of the butter, and gently fry the onion, carrot and celery until soft. Add the peas, tomatoes and courgette, and gently fry for 5 minutes.

add the asparagus, and fry for 1 minute. Stir in the cream, and simmer gently until reduced by half. Season to taste.

cook the pasta in boiling, salted, water until *al dente* or just firm to the bite. This will take about 3 minutes for fresh pasta and 10–15 minutes for dried pasta.

drain and toss with the remaining butter, the Parmesan, parsley and half of the sauce.

transfer to a serving dish, spoon the remaining sauce over the top and serve immediately.

Serves 4–6
Preparation time: *15 minutes*
Cooking time: *15–30 minutes*

Mediterranean Vegetables

with fresh herbs

4 tablespoons olive oil
1 garlic clove, crushed
3 large onions, sliced
3 large green peppers, cored, deseeded and sliced
1 x 425 g/14 oz can tomatoes
3 tablespoons chopped parsley or chervil
2 tablespoons chopped basil
2 tablespoons chopped thyme
1–2 tablespoons capers
10–12 black olives, pitted
salt and freshly ground black pepper

heat the oil in a pan, add the garlic and onions and fry very gently for 10 minutes, stirring occasionally.

add the green peppers and cook gently, stirring for 1 minute.

add the tomatoes and their juice, then the herbs and salt and pepper to taste. Bring to the boil, then lower the heat, cover and simmer for 30 minutes, stirring occasionally until the vegetables are very soft. Remove from the heat.

stir in the capers and black olives, then taste and adjust the seasoning. Serve warm, or chilled as a starter.

Serves 4
Preparation time: *20 minutes*
Cooking time: *45 minutes*

clipboard: This is a simple variation of the French vegetable dish ratatouille (see page 154), and may be served chilled in individual serving dishes as a starter. It has a rich flavour, with lots of herbs. Red peppers may be used instead of the green ones suggested here, but they will not give such a good contrast in colour.

Stir-Fried Summer Vegetables

Stir-frying is one of the healthiest ways of preparing food. It is also gratifyingly fast, so you can have delicious garden fresh vegetables from wok to table in minutes!

2 tablespoons vegetable oil

4 spring onions, trimmed and cut into 5 cm/2 inch lengths

2 garlic cloves, thinly sliced

1 cm/½ inch slice root ginger, peeled and shredded

125 g/4 oz French beans, topped, tailed and halved

½ small cauliflower, broken into florets

125 g/4 oz mangetout, topped and tailed

3 celery sticks, sliced diagonally

50 g/2 oz courgettes, sliced diagonally

1 red pepper, cored, deseeded and thinly sliced

1 green pepper, cored, deseeded and thinly sliced

1 yellow pepper, cored, deseeded and thinly sliced

2 tablespoons soy sauce

1 teaspoon sesame seed oil

freshly ground black pepper

heat the oil in a wok or large frying pan, add the spring onions and garlic and stir-fry for 30 seconds without browning.

add all the remaining vegetables, then freshly ground pepper to taste, and toss well. Stir-fry for 2 minutes.

stir in the soy sauce and sesame seed oil and serve immediately.

Serves 6
Preparation time: *35 minutes*
Cooking time: *2–3 minutes*

clipboard: To freeze, transfer the mixture to a rigid container, cool rapidly, then seal, label and freeze for up to 3 months. To cook from the freezer: leave to stand at room temperature for 3–4 hours, then turn into a wok or large frying pan. Pour over the soy sauce and sesame seed oil and stir-fry over brisk heat for 3–4 minutes until the vegetables are hot but still crisp. Serve immediately.

Winter Vegetable Casserole

with cheese topping

2 tablespoons olive oil

3 large onions, quartered

2 garlic cloves, thinly sliced

1 x 425 g/14 oz can tomatoes

150 ml/¼ pint dry white wine

1 small or ½ large celeriac, peeled and diced

4 celery sticks, trimmed and cut into 5 cm/2 inch lengths

6 carrots, quartered

1 green pepper, cored, deseeded and sliced

2 leeks, cut into 5 cm/2 inch lengths

a few cauliflower florets

1 tablespoon tomato purée

2 teaspoons dried mixed herbs

salt and freshly ground black pepper

Cheese topping

175 g/6 oz plain flour

pinch of salt

75 g/3 oz butter

2 tablespoons Parmesan cheese, freshly grated

125 g/4 oz mature Cheddar cheese, grated

2 tablespoons chopped parsley

heat the oil in a large pan, add the onion and garlic and fry gently for 5 minutes without browning, taking care not to break up the onions.

stir in the tomatoes with their juice, and wine, then add the celeriac, celery, carrots and salt and pepper to taste. Cover and simmer for 20 minutes. Stir in the green pepper, leeks, cauliflower, tomato purée and herbs and simmer for a further 10 minutes.

make the cheese topping: sift the flour and salt in a bowl. Rub in the butter until the mixture resembles fine breadcrumbs. Stir in the cheeses and parsley, then sprinkle over the vegetable mixture. Bake the casserole in a preheated oven, 200°C/400°F/Gas Mark 6, for 35–40 minutes, until golden brown. Serve hot.

Serves 4–6
Preparation time: *20 minutes*
Cooking time: *about 1¼ hours*
Oven temperature: *200°C/400°F/Gas Mark 6*

clipboard: To freeze, transfer to a rigid container, leaving 1.5 cm/¾ inch head space. Cool quickly, then seal, and freeze for up to 4 months. To thaw and serve: leave to stand in the container in the refrigerator overnight, or at room temperature for 5 hours, then transfer to a casserole or ovenproof dish.

Vegetables

Cabbage

Pak choi

Corn on
the cob

Leek

Broccoli

Red
onion

Asparagus

Onion

Shallot

Potatoes

Peas

Asparagus
Ensure that the stems are firm and the tips juicy. It is a delicious starter and is also good in sauces and soups.

Broccoli
Related to the cauliflower and cabbage, it is available in late winter and spring.

Cabbage
A highly nutritious vegetable with tightly packed leaves, it can be eaten raw in salads or cooked as an accompanying vegetable. It is available all year round.

Onion
Related to the leek and garlic, the onion can be eaten raw in salads but is more commonly cooked to add flavour.

Red onion
This mild onion is an attractive addition to salads or vegetable dishes.

Shallot
This small, mild onion can be cooked whole in casseroles and is good in delicately flavoured sauces.

Corn on the cob
Also called sweetcorn, it is best in summer and autumn. It is used to make cornflour.

Potatoes
A popular vegetable, they can be cooked in many ways. They first came to England in the 16th century with Sir Francis Drake.

Leek
Mild in flavour, this is excellent in savoury dishes, soups and salads. It has been used as the Welsh national emblem since 640AD.

Peas
Small juicy green seeds encased in a green pod, they can be served as an accompanying vegetable or as part of a casserole.

Carrots
Long root vegetables with

Fennel

Aubergine

Kabocha squash

Carrots

Globe artichokes

Courgettes

Flat mushrooms

Patty pan squash

sweet orange flesh, carrots are highly nutritious, particularly when eaten raw. They can also be cooked in casseroles or served as an accompanying vegetable.

Pak choi

Sometimes called Chinese chard or Chinese white cabbage, it is mild in flavour and can be eaten either raw or braised.

Globe artichokes

These are boiled and the leaves are pulled off one by one and served as a starter with a sauce such as vinaigrette or hollandaise.

Fennel

A bulbous plant with bright green, feathery leaves, this has a slightly aniseed flavour. Both bulb and stalks can be eaten, raw or braised.

Aubergine

Also known as eggplant, this is a fruit but is eaten as a vegetable. It can be boiled, steamed, grilled or sautéed.

Courgettes

Also known as zucchini, it has a delicate flavour, good with meat, fish or poultry. It was raised from seeds brought back by Columbus from the Americas.

Flat mushrooms

Possibly one of the oldest plants in the world, these are available all year round. There are some 250 different types of edible fungus, and flat mushrooms are the largest and have a more developed flavour. They are good in stews, vegetable dishes and soups, and go particularly well with garlic.

Kabocha squash

An edible gourd native to the Americas, it has a mild flavour and can be boiled or steamed and used in soups or stir-fries.

Patty pan squash

An American summer squash with a soft skin, it can be baked or boiled and served with butter. It has a mild flavour.

Rösti Potatoes

Everyone loves this delicious, savoury potato dish. It is warming, simple to prepare, and can be served either as a quick snack or as part of a main meal.

1 kg/2 lb potatoes, peeled and halved
or quartered if large
1 large onion, grated
1 egg, beaten
50 g/2 oz butter
salt and freshly ground black pepper

place the potatoes in a saucepan. Pour over enough water to cover and add salt. Cover, bring to the boil and simmer for 5 minutes. Drain and leave to cool.

grate the potatoes coarsely into a mixing bowl and add the grated onion. Stir in the beaten egg with salt and pepper.

heat the butter in a frying pan and add the potato mixture, spreading it over the pan. Cook over a moderate heat, turning with a spatula when the underside becomes lightly browned (there is no need to turn all the potato at once – just lift one section on to the spatula at a time and turn it over).

cook for about 15 minutes until lightly browned throughout and crisp. Use the spatula to press the potato together to form a large pancake, then cook for 2–3 minutes until the underside is browned and crisp.

turn the pancake over and cook the other side. It is easier to turn over if you invert the pancake on to a plate, then slide the pancake back into the pan to cook the other side.

serve at once, cut into wedges.

Serves 4–6
Preparation time: *10 minutes*
Cooking time: *30 minutes*

Scalloped Potatoes
flavoured with onions

1 kg/2 lb potatoes, peeled and thinly sliced
1 large onion, thinly sliced
150 ml/¼ pint Beef Stock (see page 10)
25 g/1 oz butter, melted
salt and freshly ground black pepper
1 tablespoon chopped parsley, to garnish

make layers of the potatoes and onion in a well-buttered ovenproof dish, seasoning the layers with salt and pepper.

bring the stock to the boil and pour over the potatoes, then brush liberally with the melted butter.

cover with kitchen foil and cook in a preheated oven, 180°C/350°F/Gas Mark 4, for 1½ hours.

remove the kitchen foil and cook for a further 30 minutes or until the potatoes are cooked through and lightly browned.

place under a moderate grill until the potatoes are well browned and crispy on top. Serve hot.

Serves 4–6
Preparation time: *20 minutes*
Cooking time: *about 2 hours*
Oven temperature: *180°C/350°F/Gas Mark 4*

Roast Peppers
in virgin olive oil

4 red, green and yellow peppers
4 tablespoons olive oil
1 tablespoon chopped parsley
2 garlic cloves, crushed or chopped
freshly ground sea salt

place the peppers under a hot grill and cook them until they are black and blistered. Turn them occasionally to cook them evenly on all sides. Place in a polythene bag until they are cool, and then peel away the skins.

cut the peppers open and remove the seeds. Cut the flesh into thin strips and arrange them in a serving dish.

sprinkle with olive oil and scatter with parsley and garlic. Finally, grind a little sea salt over the peppers.

Serves 4–6
Preparation time: *10 minutes*
Cooking time: *15 minutes*

Vegetable Pie
with potato pastry

Pastry
250 g/8 oz self-raising flour
175 g/6 oz butter or soft margarine
1 teaspoon salt
250 g/8 oz cold, cooked mashed potato
1 tablespoon milk
1 egg yolk, beaten

Vegetable filling
250 g/8 oz mixed vegetables, frozen or fresh, diced,
125 g/4 oz mushrooms, sliced
1 large or 2 medium onions, thinly sliced
150 ml/¼ pint Bechamel Sauce (see page 8)
75 g/3 oz Cheddar cheese, grated
salt and freshly ground black pepper

make the pastry: place the flour in a bowl, add the butter or margarine and rub in using your fingertips. Mix in the salt and work the mashed potato into this mixture, adding the milk a little at a time.

knead on a floured board until the dough is smooth and fairly soft. Roll out the pastry and use it to line a large, shallow ovenproof dish. Bake blind (see clipboard) in a preheated oven, 200°C/400°F/Gas Mark 6, for 15 minutes or until it is light golden brown.

cook the mixed vegetables in boiling salted water until just tender and allow to cool. Fry the mushrooms lightly and allow to cool. Fry the onions lightly and allow to cool. Mix the vegetables into the bechamel sauce and season to taste while the pastry is cooking.

remove the pastry from the oven, allow to cool a little and then fill with the vegetable mixture, spreading with a palette knife so that it is smooth and flat. Sprinkle with the grated Cheddar. Brush the edges of the pastry with the beaten egg yolk and return to the oven for 15 minutes or until the cheese is melted and beginning to brown. Serve hot.

Serves 4
Preparation time: *30 minutes, plus cooling*
Cooking time: *30 minutes*
Oven temperature: *200°C/400°F/Gas Mark 6*

clipboard: Baking blind is a method of pre-cooking a pastry base without a filling. After lining the dish with the pastry, prick it all over with a fork. Cut a piece of greaseproof paper to the shape of the dish and about 5 cm/2 inches larger all round, and place it over the pastry. Pour enough dried beans over the paper to cover it, then place in the oven for 15 minutes. Remove from the oven, and remove the paper and beans.

Salads and
Salad Dressings

Green Salad

with a mixed herb sauce

1 round lettuce
1 batavia lettuce
125 g/4 oz corn salad

Herb sauce
2 eggs, hard-boiled
2 tablespoons double cream
2 tablespoons olive oil
2 teaspoons white wine vinegar
1 tablespoon chopped chives
1 tablespoon chopped dill
1 tablespoon chopped tarragon
salt and freshly ground black pepper

break the round lettuce leaves in pieces and pile in a salad bowl. Using only the pale green inner leaves of the batavia lettuce, scatter them over the lettuce and put the corn salad on top.

make the herb sauce: separate the whites and yolks of the hard-boiled eggs.

chop the egg whites and scatter over the green salad. Mash the egg yolks to a paste with the cream, and stir in the oil very gradually.

add the vinegar slowly and stir until blended. Add salt and pepper to taste, and stir in the herbs.

pour the herb sauce over the salad and mix well.

Serves 4
Preparation time: *10 minutes*

clipboard: Batavia, also called escarole, is a type of endive. Though it is slightly less curly-leaved than endive, it has a similar, slightly bitter taste which provides an interesting contrast of flavour in green salads.

Waldorf Salad

with apples, celery and fresh mayonnaise

This delicious, crisp salad is deservedly praised as an American classic – it was invented at the Waldorf Astoria hotel in New York. It is popular at any time of the year, but is a special treat in winter, when fresh salad ingredients are less widely available.

4 unpeeled dessert apples, cored and diced

1 head celery, finely diced, some leaves reserved for garnish

small bunch of grapes, halved and deseeded (optional)

50 g/2 oz walnuts or pecan nuts, coarsely chopped

1 x quantity of Mayonnaise (see page 200)

mix the apples, celery, grapes and walnuts or pecan nuts, with the mayonnaise, reserving some of the nuts to garnish.

spoon into a bowl, arrange a few celery leaves around the edge and top with the remaining nuts.

Serves 4–6
Preparation time: *15–20 minutes*

Salad Leaves and Herbs

Lollo rosso

Round lettuce

Basil

*Cur.
pars*

Sage

Chicory

Marjoram

Little Gem

Lollo rosso
A dark green lettuce with attractive reddish crinkled leaves, it has a slightly bitter taste and is often used in mixed salads.

Sage
An aromatic green herb with pink and mauve flowers, it is commonly used in cheese, meat and pasta dishes. It is also a frequent ingredient in stuffings.

Round lettuce
Also known as Boston or butterhead lettuce, this has a fresh green colour and a delicate, loose leaf. It has a slightly buttery taste.

Chicory
Sometimes known as Belgian endive, this is a compact cone-shaped salad vegetable with long, yellow-tipped leaves. It can be cooked or used in salads. The roots are also roasted, ground and used as a substitute for coffee.

Marjoram
An aromatic herb, it has small, light green leaves and a spicy flavour, and can be used in any meat or vegetable dish.

Little Gem
A small, loose-leaf lettuce with pale green leaves, it has crisp, slightly crinkled leaves with no heart.

Basil
A pungent aromatic herb, it is widely used in Italian cooking. It is the main ingredient in pesto, which is a popular basil sauce often served with pasta. Basil is also used in salads, and is an attractive garnish.

Curly parsley
Also known as English parsley, this bright green herb has frilly leaves and a

Chinese leaf

Frisée

Oak leaf lettuce

Curly kale

Bay leaves

Red chicory

Rosemary

mild flavour. It is used both as a garnish and as a seasoning. It goes particularly well with salads, stews, vegetable dishes and eggs.

Curly kale

A small dark green leafy vegetable, it is related to cabbage and is cooked in exactly the same way.

Chinese leaf

These tightly packed pale green leaves have a delicate flavour and are good in salads, stir-fries or Chinese soups. It is available all year round but is considered to be at its best from early autumn to winter.

Bay leaves

Not a true herb but the leaves of the laurel tree, these are used in soups, casseroles and pasta dishes, and are an essential ingredient in *bouquet garni*.

Frisée

Also known as curly endive, this has attractive lacy leaves, which are green, white and yellow. It is a member of the chicory family and has a slightly bitter taste.

Red chicory

This has striking purplish red and white leaves. It has a sharp taste, and can be used either in salads or cooked. It makes an attractive garnish.

Rosemary

This aromatic herb is often used to flavour vinegars. It is often associated with lamb or potato dishes.

Oak leaf lettuce

A long, thin, loose-leaf lettuce with dark green leaves, it has no heart. The leaves grow loosely in a bunch and can be cut without doing any damage to the plant.

Spiced Coleslaw
with curry and paprika

Spiced dressing

3 tablespoons Mayonnaise (see page 200)
½ teaspoon curry powder
½ teaspoon ground nutmeg
½ teaspoon paprika
1 teaspoon ready-made English mustard
1 tablespoon olive oil
1 tablespoon lemon juice
salt and freshly ground black pepper

Salad

¼–½ white cabbage or cabbage heart
1 unpeeled dessert apple, cored and diced
2 carrots, grated
2 tablespoons diced gherkins
2 teaspoons capers
2 tablespoons chopped parsley

make the dressing first by blending all the ingredients together. Do this before preparing the salad so it does not become dry.

shred the cabbage finely by hand or with a food processor or blender.

add the apple and carrots to the dressing, together with the gherkins, capers and parsley. Mix together thoroughly.

Serves 4
Preparation time: *25–30 minutes*

clipboard: You should avoid making coleslaw too far ahead, as the cabbage and other ingredients should remain as fresh and crisp as possible. This is a popular salad, and the recipe can be varied in several ways. If you want a lighter dressing, substitute yogurt for the mayonnaise. If you prefer a less spicy option, omit the spices from the dressing. Children often like an extra-crunchy coleslaw, which you can make by adding chopped celery, chopped nuts, more apple and diced, fresh pineapple to the ingredients.

Bulgar salad
with lemon and oil dressing

125–150 g/4–5 oz bulgar wheat
2 tablespoons French
Dressing (see page 198)
2 tablespoons diced cucumber
1 tablespoon sliced spring onions
2 tablespoons sliced tomatoes
2 tablespoons cooked peas
2 tablespoons sweetcorn kernels
1 tablespoon chopped chives
1 tablespoon chopped mint

To garnish
pitted black olives
lemon wedges
coriander sprigs

place the wheat in a bowl. Cover it completely with boiling water and leave for 25 minutes.

drain the wheat well and place it on absorbent kitchen paper to dry.

put into a bowl with the French dressing.

add the cucumber, spring onions, tomatoes, peas, sweetcorn, chives and mint. Mix together thoroughly, garnish with black olives, lemon wedges, and coriander sprigs and serve.

Serves 4
Preparation time: *45 minutes*

clipboard: Bulgar wheat, also known as cracked wheat, gives salads and other dishes, an interesting flavour. To obtain its particular texture, the wheat has been partially cooked by boiling, then dried and cracked into small pieces. Like all wheat products, it is an excellent source of protein and fibre. To make a nourishing main meal, serve with a selection of cheeses, such as Brie, Danish Blue and Lancashire.

Roast Vegetable Salad

The flavour imparted by roasting gives vegetables a deep, seductive, smoky taste and silky texture. A range of vegetables can be prepared in this way – onions, garlic, peppers, aubergines, courgettes, fennel and artichokes are typical examples.

2 Spanish onions, unpeeled

500 g/1 lb small aubergines

2 sweet red peppers

3 firm but ripe large tomatoes

8 garlic cloves

1 teaspoon cumin seeds

3 tablespoons lemon juice

4 tablespoons virgin olive oil

3 tablespoons white wine vinegar

salt

2 tablespoons finely chopped parsley, or torn basil leaves, to garnish

place the onions on a baking sheet and bake in a preheated oven, 180°C/350°F/Gas Mark 4, for 10 minutes. Add the aubergines and bake for a further 10 minutes. Add the peppers and bake for 10 minutes before adding the tomatoes and 6 of the garlic cloves.

cook for a further 15 minutes, until all the vegetables are tender. If necessary, remove any vegetables that have cooked more quickly than the others. When the vegetables are cool enough to handle, peel them carefully with your fingers.

cut the cores and seeds from the peppers and cut the flesh into strips. Halve the tomatoes, discard the seeds and slice the flesh. Slice the aubergines into strips and the onions into rings. Arrange the peppers, tomatoes, aubergines and onions in a serving dish.

pound the roasted and raw garlic and the cumin seeds to a paste. Use a pestle and mortar or the end of a rolling pin in a small bowl. Gradually beat in the lemon juice, oil and vinegar, then add salt to taste. Pour over the vegetables and sprinkle with parsley or basil. Serve warm or cold.

Serves 4
Preparation time: *5–10 minutes*
Cooking time: *45 minutes*
Oven temperature: *180°C/350°F/Gas Mark 4*

Greek Country Salad

with black olives and feta cheese

This traditional salad immediately evokes the atmosphere of Greece! It is served in Greek tavernas all over the world.

4 tablespoons olive oil

I tablespoon red wine vinegar

I garlic clove, crushed

½ cucumber, peeled if preferred

I small round lettuce, torn

I small Cos lettuce, shredded

3 firm but ripe tomatoes, cut into wedges

I Spanish onion, thinly sliced into rings

I green pepper, cored, deseeded and thinly sliced into rings

125 g/4 oz feta cheese, crumbled

12 or more black olives, (Kalamata if possible)

salt and freshly ground black pepper

12 tablespoons coarsely chopped parsley

2 teaspoons chopped oregano

whisk together the oil, vinegar, garlic and add salt and pepper to taste. Cover and set aside for 1 hour.

halve the cucumber lengthways, scoop out the seeds and cut in thin slices. Sprinkle with salt and leave to drain.

rinse the cucumber and dry with absorbent kitchen paper.

whisk the oil and vinegar again, then toss a little of it with the lettuce in a bowl.

layer the tomatoes, cucumber, onion, green pepper, cheese and olives on the lettuce.

pour over the remaining dressing, then scatter over the chopped parsley and the oregano.

Serves 4
Preparation time: *25–30 minutes*

Salade Niçoise
Provençal salad with tuna and anchovies

I garlic clove, bruised
I lettuce
125 g/4 oz celery hearts, thinly sliced
125 g/4 oz cucumber, peeled and thinly sliced
250 g/8 oz small French beans, topped and tailed
250 g/8 oz canned artichoke hearts, thinly sliced
500 g/1 lb tomatoes, skinned (see page 20), deseeded and quartered
I large green pepper, cored, deseeded and sliced
I onion, sliced
4 eggs, hard-boiled and halved
50 g/2 oz black olives, pitted
8 canned anchovy fillets, drained
I x 250 g/8 oz can tuna fish in oil, drained

Dressing
7 tablespoons olive oil
4 basil leaves, finely chopped
salt and freshly ground black pepper

rub around the inside of a large salad bowl with the bruised garlic clove. Line the bowl with lettuce leaves.

chop the remaining lettuce leaves roughly and then arrange them in the bottom of the bowl.

mix the celery and cucumber together with the French beans and artichoke hearts. Arrange on top of the lettuce in the salad bowl.

arrange the quartered tomatoes, sliced pepper and onion, eggs, olives and anchovies on top of the mixed vegetables in the bowl.

cut the tuna into chunks and place in the bowl.

make the dressing: mix together the olive oil and chopped basil with salt and pepper to taste.

pour the dressing over the salad and transfer to individual serving plates.

Serves 4
Preparation time: *20 minutes*

Chickpea Salad
with garlic and olives

This is a delicious salad – chick peas are deservedly popular for their mild, creamy flavour, and have a wonderful affinity with olive oil and garlic.

250 g/8 oz chickpeas, dried
1 bay leaf
1 parsley sprig
1 thyme sprig
3 tablespoons olive oil
1 onion, finely chopped
2 garlic cloves, crushed
125 g/4 oz black olives, pitted
½ red onion, finely sliced
salt and freshly ground black pepper
thyme sprigs, to garnish

Vinaigrette dressing
6 tablespoons olive oil
1 tablespoon red wine vinegar
juice of ½ lemon
2 tablespoons chopped fresh herbs, such as parsley and thyme

put the chickpeas in a bowl, cover with cold water and leave to soak overnight. The following day, drain the chickpeas and rinse thoroughly under cold running water.

put the chickpeas in a saucepan and cover with fresh cold water. Add the bay leaf and sprigs of parsley and thyme.

bring to the boil, and after 10 minutes lower the heat to a bare simmer. Cook gently for about 2 hours, or until the chickpeas are tender.

drain and discard the herbs. Meanwhile, heat the olive oil in a frying pan, and add the onion and garlic.

cook gently over low heat until the onion is softened. Take care that it does not brown.

mix the vinaigrette ingredients together until thoroughly blended. Place in a bowl with the drained chickpeas and sautéed onion.

toss gently while the chickpeas are still hot, and season. Add the olives and red onion and leave to cool. Garnish and serve at room temperature.

Serves 6–8
Preparation time: *15 minutes, plus soaking*
Cooking time: *2¼ hours*

French Dressing
with variations

There are several ways to ring the changes on a basic French or vinaigrette dressing — try some of these clever variations to enhance your salads.

½ teaspoon Dijon mustard
6 tablespoons virgin olive oil
1½–2 tablespoons wine vinegar, red or white
a little sugar or honey (optional)
salt and freshly ground black or white pepper

make a basic vinaigrette dressing. Put a good pinch of salt and a shake of pepper into a bowl or jar with the mustard. Stir in the oil, then add the vinegar and taste the dressing.

adjust the seasoning to taste and blend in a little sugar or honey, if liked. The ingredients can also be blended in a liquidizer.

make a mustard vinaigrette: add an extra 1 teaspoon French or ready-made English mustard to the basic ingredients. Add a little sugar or honey to taste, in order to balance the flavour.

make a curry vinaigrette: add a pinch of curry powder or ½ teaspoon curry paste to the ingredients.

Serves 4
Preparation time: *3–4 minutes*

clipboard: The basic dressing is a vinaigrette or French dressing. Olive oil is best, but you can use partly olive and part another oil, such as corn oil. To vary the flavour, try adding a few drops of flavoured vinegar, such as raspberry, tarragon — it adds a subtle taste. The sugar or honey is not essential, but some people like a slightly sweetened dressing.

Fresh Mayonnaise

2 egg yolks (at room temperature)

1 teaspoon Dijon mustard

up to 300 ml/½ pint virgin olive oil (at room temperature)

3 teaspoons white wine vinegar or lemon juice, or a mixture of both

1 tablespoon very hot water (optional)

salt and freshly ground white pepper

make by hand: Put the egg yolks into a mixing bowl and add the mustard and salt and pepper. Whisk to blend. Hold the container of oil or mixture of oils in one hand, and leave your 'working' hand free to whisk continually.

add the oil in a very slow trickle, whisking all the time. If by any chance there is the slightest sign of the mixture curdling, stop adding the oil and whisk very hard. If that does not help, you will need to add another egg yolk.

beat this in and start adding the oil once again. The 2 egg yolks should absorb the quantity of oil specified but for many people this gives too oily a dressing, so stop when sufficient has been incorporated. Add the vinegar or vinegar and lemon juice. The hot water lightens the dressing. Use the mayonnaise at once or cover and refrigerate for 2–3 days only.

make in a liquidizer or food processor: You can use whole eggs if desired. This makes a much lighter dressing than one made with just the yolks, but it means you cannot add as much oil.

put the eggs into the goblet or bowl with the mustard, salt and pepper. Keep the motor running at the lowest speed possible. Gradually trickle in the oil through the feeding funnel, or space in the lid. When this has been incorporated, add the vinegar or lemon juice and hot water.

Serves 4–6

Preparation time: *by hand, 20 minutes; by liquidizer/food processor, 5 minutes*

clipboard: The egg yolks and oil should be at room temperature before starting to prevent the mayonnaise curdling. If you like a lighter-textured dressing, you can make the mayonnaise with a mixture of olive and sunflower or corn oils. The quantity of oil given is the maximum that the egg yolks will absorb.

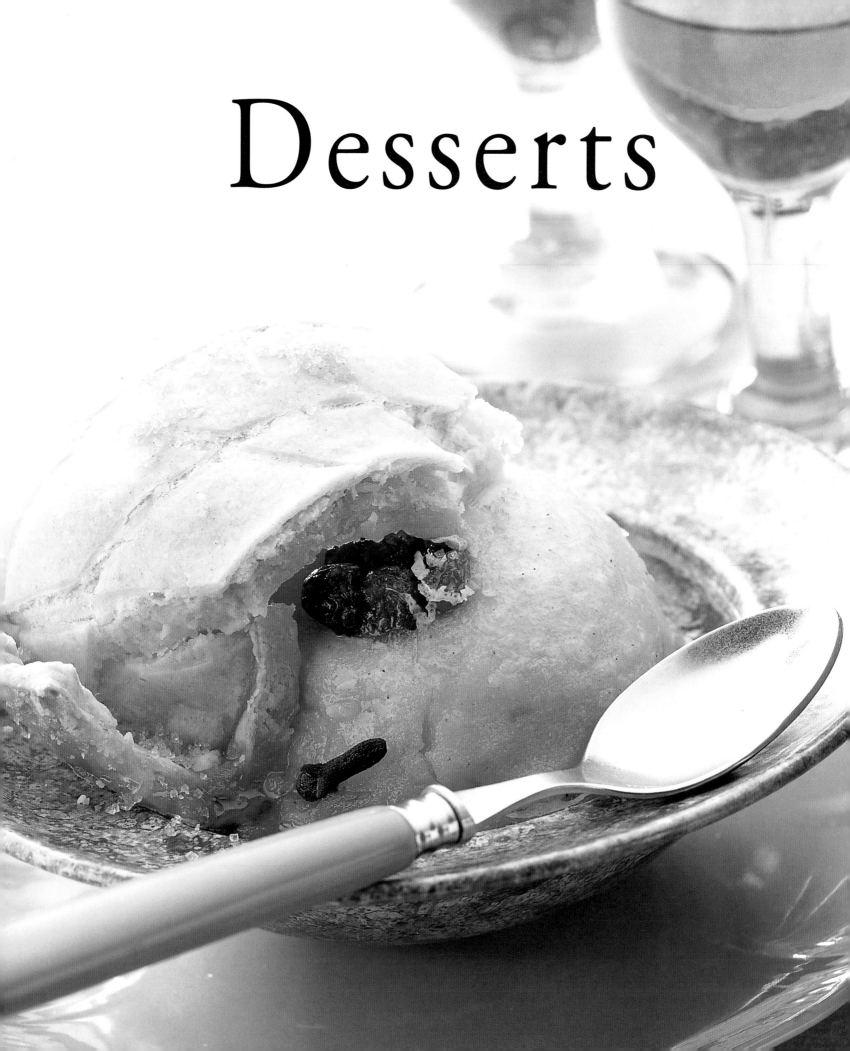

Desserts

Apple Florentine Pie *with cinnamon and ale*

This is an 18th-century recipe from Lincolnshire and Bedfordshire, traditionally made at Christmas.

Shortcrust pastry

¼ teaspoon salt
250 g/8 oz plain flour
125 g/4 oz butter or margarine
50 ml/2 fl oz very cold water

Filling

4 large cooking apples, peeled and cored
1 tablespoon grated lemon peel
3 tablespoons demerara sugar
50 g/2 oz sultanas
600 ml/1 pint pale ale
¼ teaspoon grated nutmeg
¼ teaspoon ground cinnamon
3 cloves
whipped cream, to serve

butter a deep pie dish and set aside. Make the pastry: mix the salt and flour lightly together and rub in the butter until it is the consistency of fine breadcrumbs. Mix with the cold water until a soft dough is formed. Roll out to 1 cm/½ inch thick on a floured board.

stand the apples in the pie dish and sprinkle 1 teaspoon of grated lemon peel into each one. Sprinkle 2 tablespoons of the sugar all over. Fill the centre of each apple with sultanas.

cover with the pastry and bake in a preheated oven, 200°C/400°F/Gas Mark 6, for 30 minutes.

heat together, but do not boil, the ale, nutmeg, cinnamon, cloves and the remaining sugar.

loosen the crust carefully and lift the pastry off the apples. Pour the ale mixture over the apples. Cut the pastry into 4 pieces and place one on each apple. Serve very hot in bowls, topped with whipped cream.

Serves 4
Preparation time: *30 minutes*
Cooking time: *30 minutes*
Oven temperature: *200°C/400°F/Gas Mark 6*

Summer Fruit

Granny Smith

Strawberries

Nectarine 'Big John'

Nectarine 'Sunlite'

Golden Delicious

Cox's Orange Pippin

Blackberries

Raspberries

Blueberries

Granny Smith

The Granny Smith was originally an Australian apple. It is both crisp and juicy, and has a bright green skin and particularly sweet-tasting flesh.

Cox's Orange Pippin

This is one of the most popular English apples. It has a fresh-looking green and red skin and a medium soft flesh with a sweet, slightly acid flavour.

Blackberries

These are the small, purplish black, juicy berries of the bramble or blackberry bush. Blackberries are at their best picked fresh in the late summer and early autumn, and are particularly good in jams and pies.

Golden Delicious

This a French apple with soft, pale greenish yellow skin. It has soft flesh and a mild flavour.

Strawberries

Related to the rose, the strawberry bush bears red juicy berries with seed-pitted skin and small green leaves. Strawberries have a delicate, sweet taste. They are delicious served by themselves or with cream, in jams, ice cream, tarts and pies. They also make an attractive garnish. Strawberries are at their best in the summer.

Raspberries

The raspberry is the soft pinkish red fruit of the thorn bush, which is related to the rose. It a delicious fruit, eaten either with cream or ice cream or puréed for use in pies or tarts. Originally from northern Europe, raspberries are available in mid-summer through to the autumn. They freeze well.

Nectarines

Related to the peach, the nectarine has smooth, yellowish red skin and a

Plums

Apricots

Cherries

Pear 'Rocha'

Pear 'Comice'

Redcurrants

sweet golden flesh surrounding a large stone. It can be eaten on its own or used in fruit salad. Two popular varieties of nectarine are 'Big John' and 'Sunlite'. They are at their best in late summer.

Blueberries

A small soft purple-blue berry from North America, the blueberry is sometimes known as a huckleberry. It has a mild, sweet taste and is good for use in jams, pies or eaten fresh.

Plums

Round, shiny fruit ranging in colour from yellow to purple, plums have sweet flesh with a single flat stone. This variety is the Santa Rose, which is good raw, in a fruit salad, or stewed.

Apricots

The apricot is the same size as the plum but golden in colour with a similar flavour to the peach. It can be eaten raw on its own, or cooked, when it has a tart, tangy flavour and is used in both sweet and savoury dishes.

Redcurrants

They can be eaten fresh, though they are sometimes tart, and are excellent in jams, sauces and as a garnish.

Cherries

These are small, round, juicy fruits with a single stone, which range from tart to sweet in taste. Available in the early summer months, they can be eaten raw, in pies, in preserves, or with some meat dishes – in particular duck.

Pears

The pear, which originated in Asia, is a yellow, green or brown, soft-skinned fruit. It has juicy, sweet white flesh. It is good eaten by itself, in fruit salad, or poached in syrup or wine. Pears are at their best in early summer to late autumn. Two of the most common varieties are the Comice and the Rocha, shown here.

Fruit Compôte
with summer garden fruits

Nothing is easier to make or more delicious to eat than this simple dessert. It has all the fresh flavours and jewel colours of traditional garden fruits.

500 g/1 lb mixed redcurrants, blackcurrants and blackberries, washed
125 g/ 4 oz caster sugar
250 g/ 8 oz raspberries
whipped cream, to serve

place the currants and blackberries in a heavy pan with the sugar. Cook gently over a low heat, stirring occasionally, for 10 minutes until tender.

remove from the heat, add the raspberries, and set aside to cool.

spoon into individual serving bowls and serve with whipped cream.

Serves 6
Preparation time: *10 minutes, plus cooling*
Cooking time: *10 minutes*

Traditional Rice Pudding

scented with with rosewater

A perfectly made rice pudding is a true delicacy, so it is worthwhile knowing how to make it. This recipe has an exquisite balance of flavour and texture. Pure bliss!

75g/3 oz pudding rice
125 g/4 oz sugar
½ teaspoon ground nutmeg
¼ teaspoon ground coriander
½ teaspoon salt
2 tablespoons grated suet
600 ml/1 pint milk
4 egg yolks, plus 1 egg white
4 tablespoons fresh white breadcrumbs
2 tablespoons rosewater
brown sugar, to serve
lemon peel, cut into slivers, to decorate (optional)

combine the rice, sugar, spices, salt, suet and milk in a saucepan.

cook over low heat, stirring occasionally, for about 30 minutes, or until the mixture is thick and creamy.

beat in the egg yolks and the egg white, the breadcrumbs and rosewater until thoroughly blended. Serve warm, sprinkled with brown sugar and decorated with slivers of lemon peel, if liked.

Serves 4
Preparation time: *10 minutes*
Cooking time: *30–35 minutes*

Treacle Pudding
with hot treacle sauce

Treacle pudding is one of the great British traditions, and tastes absolutely wonderful. Steamed to a light, fluffy texture, it readily absorbs the delicious, aromatic sauce.

125 g/4 oz butter or margarine, plus extra for basin
125 g/4 oz caster sugar
2 large eggs
125 g/4 oz self-raising flour, sifted
4 tablespoons golden syrup

Treacle sauce
4 tablespoons golden syrup
1 tablespoon water

butter a 900 ml/1½ pint pudding basin.

cream the butter or margarine and sugar together in a bowl until light and fluffy. Beat in the eggs, 1 at a time, adding a little of the flour with the second egg. Fold in the remaining flour.

spoon 4 tablespoons of golden syrup into the buttered pudding basin, then put the sponge mixture on top.

cover with buttered foil, making a pleat across the centre to allow the pudding to rise. Steam for 1½–2 hours.

make the sauce: heat the syrup and water in a small pan. Turn out the pudding on to a warmed serving dish and pour over the hot sauce just before serving.

Serves 4
Preparation time: *20–30 minutes*
Cooking time: *1½–2 hours*

Coffee and Brandy Ice Cream

3 eggs
75 g/3 oz caster sugar
300 ml/½ pint single cream
3 tablespoons instant coffee powder
300 ml/½ pint double cream
3 tablespoons brandy

beat the eggs and sugar together until smooth. Bring the single cream and coffee just to the boil in a small pan, then stir into the egg mixture.

transfer to the top of a double boiler, or to a heatproof bowl over a pan of simmering water.

cook gently, stirring constantly, until the custard is thick enough to coat the back of a spoon.

strain into a bowl and leave to cool, stirring occasionally to prevent a skin forming.

whip the double cream until it will stand in soft peaks, then fold into the cold custard with the brandy.

pour into a rigid container, cover and freeze for 2–3 hours until half-frozen. Remove from the freezer and stir well, then return to the container.

seal and label, then return to the freezer for up to 3 months. Transfer the ice cream to the refrigerator 30 minutes before serving to allow it to soften.

scoop into chilled glasses or dishes and serve immediately.

Serves 6–8
Preparation time: *20 minutes, plus freezing*

Exotic Fruit

Water melon

Papaya

Canteloupe melon

Clementine

Mandarin

Orange

Mango

Lychees

Kiwi fruit

Grapes

Tamarillo

Water melon
Its sweet, juicy red flesh can be eaten on its own or used in drinks, sorbets or salads.

Lychees
A native of China, lychees have a grape-like flavour and are used in fruit salads and savoury dishes. They are at their best in summer.

Canteloupe melon
Probably the most famous dessert melon, it has sweet, pale orange flesh.

Kiwi fruit
Also known as the Chinese gooseberry, it has sweet, juicy green flesh and black pips. It can be eaten by itself or used in fruit salad or sorbets.

Papaya
Also known as the paw paw, it has orange flesh and dark seeds, in season in summer.

Native to the US, it is eaten by itself or in fruit salad.

Mango
It has sweet golden flesh and a large single seed. In season in summer, it can be eaten by itself or used in curries, chutney or ice cream.

Clementine
Grown mainly in Mediterranean countries, it has sweet juicy flesh and

firm skin. It can be eaten by itself or used in dessert dishes, pickles and vinegars.

Grapes
Grapes can be dried to make currants or sultanas. They are also delicious eaten on their own.

Tamarillo
Native to Peru, this has sharp-tasting flesh, used in sweet and savoury dishes.

Mandarin
Also called a tangerine, it is a small fruit of the orange family, with a loose orange skin and sweet juicy flesh.

Orange
This is the best known of all the citrus fruits and can be eaten either on its own or in fruit salads. Both the juice and the rind can also be used to add flavour to sweet and savoury dishes.

Bananas

Persimmon

Pink grapefruit

Pineapple

Lemon

Custard apple

Grapefruit

Mangosteen

Lime

Pomegranate

Physalis

Kumquats

Kumquats

This tiny citrus fruit, from Brazil, has a sweet-and-sour taste and is eaten unpeeled. It can be candied.

Grapefruit

Larger than the orange and sharper in taste, it has yellow skin. It is eaten by itself, often with sugar.

Pink grapefruit

This grapefruit has pink flesh.

Lime

Its sour juice is used in desserts and savoury dishes. It is refreshing in drinks.

Lemon

Available all year round, its juice and rind are used in sweet and savoury dishes.

Mangosteen

It has soft white flesh similar to that of the lychee. It is eaten by itself.

Persimmon

It has soft, sweet, golden flesh. It can be eaten by itself or in fruit salad. Native to Japan and China, it is in season in the late autumn and early winter.

Physalis

Also known as the cape gooseberry, this is a small orange berry with a papery husk. The fruit is sweet and juicy and is eaten whole.

Custard apple

Originally from Peru, it has juicy white flesh and a sweet and sour flavour with a rose-like scent. The chilled fruit is cut in half, the black seeds are removed, and it is usually eaten with a spoon. It can also be eaten in fruit salads and sorbets.

Pineapple

Its yellow flesh is sweet and juicy and is good on its own or added to savoury or sweet dishes. It is best in spring.

Banana

It has soft, starchy flesh and can be eaten by itself or used in sweet or savoury dishes.

Pomegranate

The juice is used to make grenadine, and the seeds are used in fruit salad and ice cream. From Asia, it is in season in late autumn.

Raspberry Sorbet

500 g/1 lb raspberries, fresh or frozen
125 g/4 oz sugar
300 ml/½ pint water
2 egg whites

thaw the raspberries at room temperature for 3–4 hours if you are using them from the freezer.

pass the raspberries through a sieve. Put the sugar and water in a saucepan and stir over a gentle heat until the sugar has dissolved.

increase the heat and boil briskly, without stirring, for 8 minutes or until a syrup has formed. Allow to cool.

stir the syrup into the raspberry purée and pour into an ice tray or shallow rigid container.

place in the freezer for 1 hour or until just smooth. Whisk the egg whites until stiff and fold into the raspberry mixture.

return to the container. Cover and seal, then return to the freezer.

to serve: thaw, covered, in the refrigerator for 10–15 minutes, or microwave uncovered on Defrost for 2–3 minutes. stand 3 minutes before serving.

Serves 4–6
Preparation time: *10 minutes, plus freezing*

clipboard: If you have a glut of fresh raspberries from your garden, make this recipe in the summer, and you will have a delicious sorbet available throughout the year at very little cost. For a special occasion, pour a little liqueur, such as Cointreau, over each serving.

Iced Chocolate Mousse *with whipped cream*

4 eggs, separated
125 g/4 oz caster sugar
125 g/4 oz plain chocolate, broken into small pieces
3 tablespoons water
300 ml/½ pint double cream
8 tablespoons double cream, whipped,
to decorate

put the egg yolks and sugar in a bowl and whisk with an electric beater until the mixture is thick and fluffy.

melt the chocolate with the water in a heatproof bowl over a pan of hot water. Remove from the heat and cool slightly.

whisk this into the egg mixture. Whip the cream until it will stand in soft peaks, then carefully it fold into the chocolate mixture.

whisk the egg whites until stiff, carefully fold 1 tablespoon into the mousse, then fold in the remainder.

pour the mousse mixture into 8 individual dishes and chill. Serve with whipped cream.

Serves 8
Preparation time: *10–12 minutes, plus chilling*

clipboard: These mousses can be frozen until required. Pour the mousse mixture into freezer-proof dishes, cover them with clingfilm, wrap in polythene bags, then seal, label and freeze for up to 3 months. To thaw and serve, unwrap the mousses, and pipe a rosette of cream on top of each one. Place in the refrigerator for 10 minutes before serving until they are slightly softened.

Coffee Meringues

Meringues

2 egg whites
125 g/4 oz caster sugar
1 tablespoon instant coffee powder

Coffee cream filling

250–300 ml/8–10 fl oz double cream
2 tablespoons Tia Maria or other
coffee-flavoured liqueur
pistachios or almonds, toasted, to decorate

line 2 baking sheets with non-stick paper or baking parchment.

draw six 7.5 cm/3 inch circles and six 5 cm/2 inch circles on the paper with a pencil.

whisk the egg whites until stiff, then whisk in the sugar 1 tablespoon at a time. Add the coffee powder and continue whisking until the meringue is very stiff and holds its shape.

spoon into a piping bag fitted with a 1 cm/½ inch plain nozzle and pipe over the circles.

bake in a preheated cool oven, 110°C/225°F/Gas Mark ¼, for 1½ hours until crisp. Peel the paper carefully off the meringues, then cool on a rack.

whip the cream and liqueur together in a bowl until stiff. Spoon into a piping bag fitted with a large fluted nozzle and pipe three-quarters of the cream on to the larger meringue circles.

top with the small circles, then pipe a whirl on each one with the remaining cream to serve. Decorate with toasted pistachios or almonds.

Serves 6
Preparation time: *35–40 minutes*
Cooking time: *1½ hours*
Oven temperature: *110°C/225°F/Gas Mark ¼*

clipboard: To freeze, open-freeze the meringues until solid, then pack carefully in a rigid container, separating each one with an interleaving sheet of kitchen foil. Seal, label and return to the freezer for up to 3 months. To thaw and serve, place the meringues on a serving plate and leave to stand at room temperature for 2 hours. Serve as soon as possible.

Gâteau Ganache
with chocolate cream filling

Meringues

4 egg whites
275 g/9 oz caster sugar
few drops of vanilla essence
1 teaspoon white wine vinegar
125 g/4 oz hazelnuts, ground and toasted

Filling

75 g/3 oz plain chocolate, broken into small pieces
3 tablespoons water
300 ml/½ pint double cream

To decorate

25 g/1 oz plain chocolate
2–3 physalis (optional)

grease two 20 cm/8 inch sandwich tins, line the bases with greaseproof paper, then grease the paper.

whisk the egg whites until stiff, then whisk in the sugar, 1 tablespoon at a time. Continue whisking until the meringue is very stiff and holds its shape. Carefully fold in the vanilla essence, vinegar and hazelnuts.

turn the mixture into the prepared tins and level the surface. Bake in a preheated oven, 180°C/350°F/Gas Mark 4, for 45–50 minutes. Loosen the meringues from the tins with a sharp knife, turn out and carefully peel off the paper. Place on a wire rack and leave to cool.

melt the chocolate with the water in a heatproof bowl over a pan of hot water. Remove from the heat and leave to cool.

whip the cream until it begins to thicken, then whisk in the cooled chocolate and continue whisking until stiff. Sandwich the meringue rounds together with the chocolate cream.

decorate the meringue: melt the 25 g/1 oz chocolate in a heatproof bowl over a pan of hot water, remove from the heat and leave to cool.

put the cooled chocolate in a greaseproof piping bag, snip off the tip, then drizzle the chocolate across the top of the meringue. Leave to set. Decorate with physalis, if liked, and serve as soon as possible.

Serves 6–8
Preparation time: *45–50 minutes*
Cooking time: *45–50 minutes*
Oven temperature: *180°C/350°F/Gas Mark 4*

Baked Ricotta Cheesecake

50g/2 oz butter or margarine
175 g/6 oz digestive biscuits, crushed
250 g/8 oz ricotta cheese
2 eggs, separated
50 g/2 oz almonds, ground
rind of 1 finely grated lemon
150 ml/¼ pint single cream
50 g/2 oz caster sugar

To decorate
a little icing sugar
slivers of lemon rind

oil a 20 cm/8 inch springform cake tin.

melt the butter in a small pan, then mix in the biscuit crumbs. Press the mixture over the base of the cake tin, then chill in the refrigerator for about 15 minutes until firm.

beat the ricotta cheese with the egg yolks, almonds and lemon rind until smooth, then gradually stir in the cream.

whisk the egg whites until stiff, then whisk in the sugar a little at a time. Carefully fold into the cheese mixture, then spoon over the biscuit base and level the surface.

bake in a preheated oven, 160°C/325°F/Gas Mark 3, for 1–1¼ hours until firm. Turn off the heat and leave the cheesecake in the oven until cold. Put in the refrigerator and chill. To serve, dust with a sifted icing sugar and sprinkle with lemon rind.

Serves 8
Preparation time: *40 minutes*
Cooking time: *1–1¼ hours*
Oven temperature: *160°C/325°F/Gas Mark 3*

clipboard: To freeze, open-freeze the cheesecake until solid, then remove from the tin and place on a cake board. Wrap in a polythene bag, seal, label and return to the freezer for up to 1 month. To thaw and serve: unwrap, place on a serving plate and leave to stand in the refrigerator overnight. Sift icing sugar over the top of the cheesecake just before serving. Serve chilled.

Tipsy Cake

with sweet wine

Tipsy cakes were traditionally served at supper dances, evoking images of scenes from a Jane Austen novel. This 18th-century recipe is beautifully decorative.

1 large sponge cake or 8 small ones
3 tablespoons apricot jam
350 ml/12 fl oz sweet sherry or Madeira or Marsala
3 tablespoons orange juice, strained
75 g/3 oz caster sugar
600 ml/1 pint double cream
250 g/8 oz blanched almonds, split and toasted

cut the cake into 8 sections and stick them back together with apricot jam, or stick the 8 small cakes together.

cut out a well in the top of the cake, reserving the piece that has been cut out to put back later. Fill the well with wine and pour the remaining wine all over the cake.

chill in the refrigerator overnight, spooning the wine over the cake from time to time. Replace the reserved piece of cake the next day.

whip the orange juice, sugar and cream until soft peaks form and spoon over the cake.

arrange the almonds in a decorative pattern over the cake. Serve immediately.

Serves 8
Preparation time: *45 minutes, plus chilling overnight*

Apple Pie
with almond pastry

Pastry

175 g/6 oz plain flour
2 rounded tablespoons ground almonds
125 g/4 oz butter, at room temperature
25 g/1 oz icing sugar, sifted
1 egg yolk
2 tablespoons cold water
a little milk for glazing

Fruit filling

750 g/1½ lb apples, peeled, cored and sliced, or
500g/1 lb apples and 250 g/8 oz blackberries
2 teaspoons lemon juice
125 g/4 oz caster sugar

To serve

clotted cream

make the pastry: put the flour and almonds into a basin, then add the butter. Cut into small pieces and rub into the flour with your fingertips. Add the sifted icing sugar. Mix well. Make a well in the centre and put the egg yolk and water mixed together into it. Mix to a rough dough in the basin with a fork.

turn on to a lightly floured surface and knead gently until the dough is quite smooth. Roll into a ball and chill for at least 30 minutes before using. If using blackberries, put them into a dish and place in the oven while it is heating up.

divide the pastry into 2 halves and roll out to fit a 20 cm/8 inch shallow pie plate and line it with one half of the pastry. Fill the pie with the apples (or blackberries and apples), the lemon juice, about 3–4 tablespoons of blackberry juice, if using, from the warmed dish, and the sugar. Moisten the edges and lay the other piece of pastry on top, pressing down the edges with finger and thumb.

make a small slit in the middle to let the air out, or prick lightly all over the top, and brush with a little milk.

bake in the centre of the preheated oven, 200°C/400°F/Gas Mark 6, for 20 minutes, then reduce the oven temperature to 160°C/325°F/Gas Mark 3 and bake for a further 15–20 minutes. Serve warm with clotted cream.

Serves 4–6
Preparation time: *50 minutes*
Cooking time: *40 minutes*
Oven temperature: *200°C/400°F/Gas Mark 6*, then *160°C/325°F/Gas Mark 3*

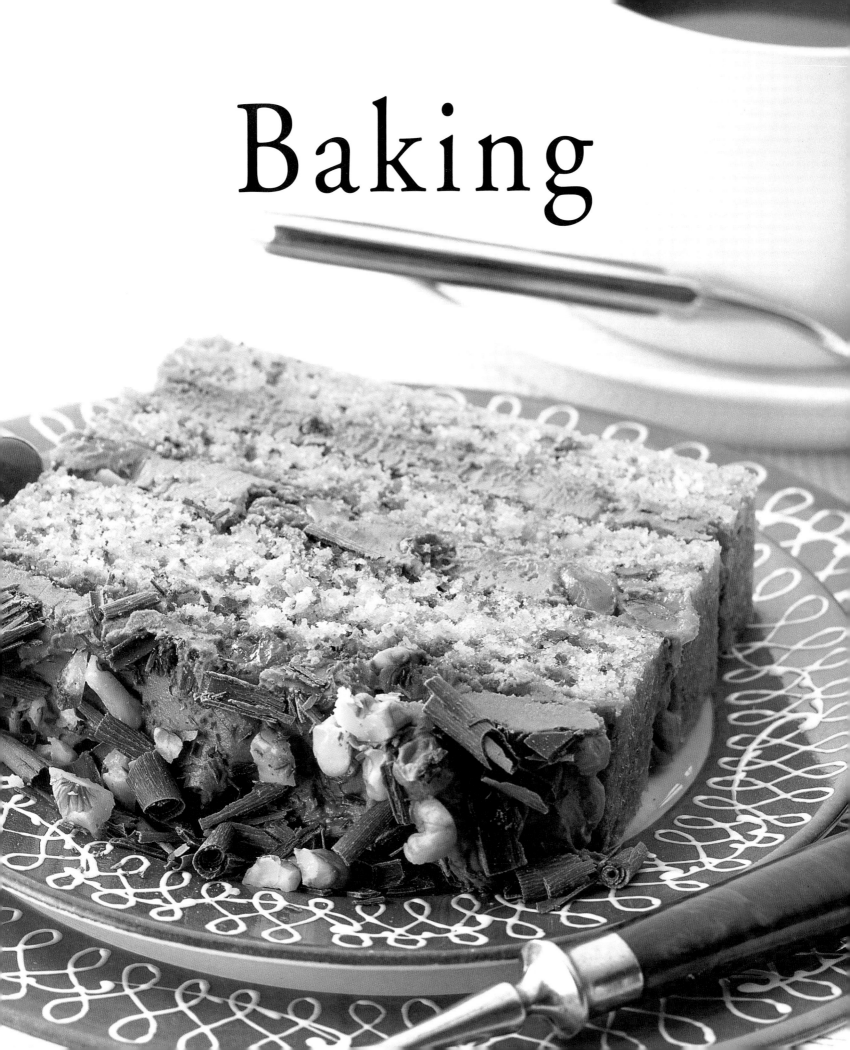

Baking

Wholemeal Bread

750 g/1½ lb strong wholemeal flour
1 teaspoon salt
25 g/1 oz butter or margarine or
1 tablespoon olive or other oil
1 sachet of 'instant' dried yeast
480 ml/just over ¾ pint water
1 tablespoon sugar

grease two 500 g/1 lb bread tins if you are making tin loaves, or 2 baking trays if you are making bloomer loaves. Sift the flour and salt into a large bowl. Rub in the butter or margarine, or add the oil. Add the yeast to the flour. Heat the water to about 43°C/110°F (tepid). An easy way to do this is to boil half the amount, and top it up with cold water. Add the sugar, and stir into the flour mixture.

turn this mixture out on to a lightly floured working surface, and knead thoroughly. To do this, fold the dough towards you, then push it away. Continue like this until the dough is firm and elastic, and no longer feels sticky. This stage can be done with the dough hook in an electric mixer. Test if the dough is ready by pressing firmly with a floured finger. This will leave an impression, but if it fades out, the dough has been kneaded enough. Do not over-knead the dough, as this spoils the bread – test frequently, especially if you are using a machine.

prove the dough – i.e. let it rise: return the dough to the mixing bowl and cover with a cloth. As it will rise to double its original bulk, it needs plenty of space. Put the dough in a warm place, e.g. an airing cupboard, and leave it to rise for 1 hour (or 2–2½ hours in a cooler spot).

knock back (knead) the dough again. To make 2 tin loaves, divide the dough into 2 halves, and press out into neat oblongs the same length and 3 times the width of the tins. Fold to fit the tins and place the dough inside them with the fold underneath.

cover the dough lightly and leave until nearly double in size. This takes from 20 minutes. Bake in a preheated oven, 220°C/425°F/Gas Mark 7, for approximately 35 minutes. To test if the bread is cooked, knock the bottom of the loaf – it should sound hollow.

Makes 2 loaves
Preparation time: *40–50 minutes, plus 1–3 hours rising*
Cooking time: *35 minutes*
Oven temperature: *220°C/425°F/Gas Mark 7*

Fresh Bread Rolls

There is nothing nicer than the smell of freshly baked bread — other than eating it! These fragrant little rolls are easy to make, and taste scrumptious.

15 g/½ oz fresh yeast
450 ml/¾ pint warm water
750 g/1½ lb plain, strong white flour
15 g/½ oz lard
milk to glaze

blend the yeast with one-third of the water.

sift the flour into a large bowl and rub in the lard. Make a well in the centre and pour in the yeast liquid, plus the remaining water.

mix to a soft dough, then work with one hand until the dough leaves the sides of the bowl clean.

turn on to a lightly floured surface and knead for 10 minutes, until smooth and elastic. Place in a clean, warmed bowl, cover with a damp cloth and leave to rise in a warm place for about 1 hour or until the dough has doubled in size.

turn out and knead for 2–3 minutes, then divide into 18 pieces. Shape into rounds and place 2.5 cm/1 in apart on floured baking sheets. Cover with clingfilm and leave to rise until doubled in size.

brush with a little milk and bake in a preheated oven, 230°C/450° F/Gas Mark 8, for 20 minutes. Transfer to a wire rack to cool.

Makes 18 rolls
Preparation time: *25 minutes, plus rising*
Cooking time: *20 minutes*
Oven temperature: *230°C/450°F/Gas Mark 8*

Baked Scones

with whipped cream

250 g/8 oz plain flour

1 teaspoon cream of tartar

½ teaspoon bicarbonate of soda

pinch of salt

50 g/2 oz butter or margarine

25 g/1 oz caster sugar

125 ml/4 fl oz milk (approximately)

extra milk to glaze

To serve

butter or whipped cream

jam

sift the flour, cream of tartar, soda and salt into a mixing bowl and rub in the fat with your fingertips until the mixture resembles breadcrumbs. Stir in the sugar and add enough milk to mix to a soft dough.

turn on to a floured surface, knead lightly and roll out to 2 cm/1¾ inch thick. Cut into 5 cm/2 inch rounds.

place on a floured baking sheet and brush with milk.

bake in a preheated oven, 220°C/425°F/Gas Mark 7, for 10 minutes. Transfer to a wire rack to cool. Serve with butter and jam or with whipped cream and jam.

Makes about 10

Preparation time: *10 minutes*

Cooking time: *10 minutes*

Oven temperature: 220°C/425°F/Gas Mark 7

Bath Buns

These light, sugary buns are thought to be the invention of the famous Dr Oliver of Bath. He was also responsible for creating the Bath Oliver biscuit.

15 g/½ oz fresh yeast or 5 g/¼ oz dried yeast
1 teaspoon sugar
300 ml/½ pint tepid milk
375 g/12 oz plain flour
125 g/4 oz butter
75 g/3 oz caster sugar
2 eggs, beaten
50 g/2 oz candied peel, chopped
50 g/2 oz lump sugar, crushed

cream the yeast with the sugar and add to the tepid milk. (If using dried yeast, mix with the sugar and half the milk. Leave in a warm place until frothy, then add the rest of the milk.)

put the flour in a bowl and pour the yeast mixture into a well in the middle. Leave until frothy.

cream the butter and sugar, add the eggs, reserving a little to glaze, and work into the dough.

reserve a little peel for decoration, then add the rest to the dough.

cover the dough with a cloth and leave in a warm place to rise for about 40 minutes.

turn out and knead, then shape into buns about 5–7.5 cm/2–3 inches across and place on a greased baking sheet, well spaced out.

leave to rise for a further 15–20 minutes, then brush with the rest of the egg, sprinkle with the coarsely crushed sugar and a little chopped peel.

bake in a preheated oven, 180°C/350°F/Gas Mark 4, for about 30 minutes. Transfer to a wire rack to cool.

Makes about 10
Preparation time: *25 minutes, plus rising*
Cooking time: *30 minutes*
Oven temperature: *180°C/350°F/Gas Mark 4*

Devonshire Splits

Served with clotted cream and jam, these are the basis of the famous Devonshire cream tea. When served with clotted cream and black treacle, they are known as 'Thunder and Lightning'.

15 g/½ oz fresh yeast or 5g/¼ oz dried yeast
½ teaspoon caster sugar
150 ml/¼ pint tepid water
25 g/1 oz lard
50 g/2 oz butter
6 tablespoons milk
500 g/1 lb plain flour
pinch of salt

To serve
icing sugar
clotted cream or whipped cream
jam

sprinkle the fresh yeast and sugar over the tepid water and leave until it is frothy. (If using dried yeast, mix with the sugar and tepid water and leave in a warm place for about 10 minutes, until it becomes frothy.)

put the lard, butter and milk into a small saucepan and heat gently until the fats have melted, but on no account let it boil. Remove from the heat and allow to cool.

meanwhile, sift the flour and salt into a mixing bowl, make a well in the centre and pour in the yeast and milk mixtures, then mix with your fingers until it is soft but not sticky.

turn on to a floured surface and knead gently for 5 minutes, then put into a bowl and leave, covered, in a warm place for 1 hour.

take out and knead again a little, then shape into about 18 small balls. Place them on a greased baking sheet a little apart, and leave until they have spread and are just touching.

bake in preheated oven, 200°C/400°F/Gas Mark 6, for about 20 minutes or until risen. When cooked, they should sound hollow when tapped. Dust with icing sugar, and serve with clotted cream and jam.

Makes about 18 buns
Preparation time: *25 minutes, plus rising*
Cooking time: *20 minutes*
Oven temperature: *200°C/400°F/Gas Mark 6*

Carrot Cake

There are many recipes for carrot cake, which is also sometimes called Passion cake. This gives a delightfully moist yet light cake with a pleasing flavour.

175 g/6 oz butter or margarine

175 g/6 oz soft brown sugar

3 large eggs

175 g/6 oz wholemeal self-raising flour or plain flour sifted with 1½ teaspoons baking powder

50 g/2 oz ground almonds

175 g/6 oz young carrots, finely grated

75 g/3 oz walnuts, coarsely chopped

1 tablespoon milk

To decorate

375 g/12 oz Quark or curd cheese (optional)

2 tablespoons halved or chopped walnuts (optional)

grease and flour or line a 20 cm/8 inch cake tin.

cream the butter or margarine and sugar until soft and light. Beat the eggs and gradually blend into the creamed mixture.

fold in the flour, or flour and baking powder, with the ground almonds.

add the carrots, walnuts and milk. Mix thoroughly, then spoon into the prepared tin.

bake for 1 hour in a preheated oven, 180°C/350°F/Gas Mark 4, or until firm to the touch. Cool for 5 minutes in the tin.

decorate when cool, if liked. Split the cake through the centre and spread with a good layer of cheese.

top with the rest of the cheese and scatter with chopped or halved walnuts.

Serves 8
Preparation time: *15 minutes*
Cooking time: *1 hour*
Oven temperature: *180°C/350°F/Gas Mark 4*

clipboard: Quark, the slightly acidic German soft cheese, makes an excellent filling and topping for this carrot cake. Quark is generally available at large supermarkets.

Chocolate Gâteau
with rum and walnuts

Walnut-crumb sponge
175 g/6 oz butter

175 g/6 oz caster sugar

3 large eggs

1 tablespoon rum

100 g/4 oz self-raising flour, sifted with ½ teaspoon baking powder or plain flour with 1½ teaspoons baking powder

40 g/1½ oz walnuts, finely chopped

40 g/1½ oz digestive biscuits, crushed

Filling
75 g/3 oz sultanas

3 tablespoons rum

175 g/6 oz plain or bitter chocolate

150 g/5 oz icing sugar

150 g/5 oz butter

50 g/2 oz walnuts, coarsely chopped

line a 1 kg/2½ lb loaf tin with greaseproof paper or baking parchment.

cream the butter and sugar until soft and light. Beat the eggs with the rum. Gradually beat the eggs and rum into the creamed mixture, adding a little flour and baking powder if the mixture shows signs of curdling. When all the eggs and rum have been incorporated, add the rest of the flour, the nuts and crumbs.

spoon into the tin and bake in a preheated oven, 180°C/350°F/Gas Mark 4, for approximately 45 minutes, or until firm to the touch. Cool for about 10 minutes in the tin, then turn out and allow to cool. Split into 3 layers.

soak the sultanas in the rum for the filling and topping, while the sponge is cooking.

melt 150 g/5 oz of the chocolate and coarsely grate the remainder. Sift the icing sugar and cream with the butter. Add the melted chocolate and beat until light in texture. Add the sultanas, rum and half the walnuts.

sandwich the layers with some of the chocolate and rum mixture. Spread the remainder over the top, but not the sides of the gâteau. Sprinkle the last of the walnuts and the grated chocolate over the top of the icing. Chill well before serving.

Serves 6–8

Preparation time: *45 minutes*

Cooking time: *45 minutes*

Oven temperature: *180°C/350°F/Gas Mark 4*

Rich Fruit Cake

Group A ingredients
250 g/8 oz plain flour
¾ teaspoon ground cinnamon
¾ teaspoon mixed spice

Group B ingredients
175 g/6 oz butter
175g/6 oz moist brown sugar
¾ tablespoon black treacle or syrup
1½ teaspoons lemon rind

Group C ingredients
4 large eggs
1½ tablespoons sherry or rum or brandy

Group D ingredients
75 g/3 oz candied peel, chopped
75 g/3 oz blanched almonds, chopped
75 g/3 oz glacé cherries, quartered
375 g/12 oz currants
250 g/8 oz sultanas
175 g/6 oz seedless raisins

decide on the shape of cake required. This quantity is sufficient for a 20 cm/8 inch round tin or an 18 cm/7 inch square tin.

line the selected cake tin carefully. Put brown paper, then greased greaseproof paper or baking parchment on the base of the tin. Place a band of greased greaseproof paper or baking parchment around the inside. Finally, tie a deep band of brown paper around the outside of the tin; this should come well above the top.

assemble all the ingredients together, and divide them into groups A,B,C and D.

mix the ingredients in the following order: sift the flour and spices together (group A). Cream the ingredients in group B until soft.

beat the eggs and alcohol together (group C) and beat this gradually into the creamed mixture. If this shows signs of curdling, beat in a little of the flour mixture. Stir in all the flour, then all the fruit ingredients from group D. Blend well, but do not beat the mixture too much.

spoon the cake mixture into the prepared tin and spread it level. Then press the mixture with damp, not wet knuckles – this helps to keep the top of the cake from becoming too hard.

place the tin in a preheated oven, 160°C/325°F/Gas Mark 3, and bake for 1¼ hours. Reduce the temperature to 140°–150°C/275°–300°F/Gas Mark 1–2, and bake for 1¾ hours. Allow the cake to cool in the tin.

Serves 6–8
Preparation time: *30 minutes*
Cooking time: *3 hours*
Oven temperature: *160°C/325°F/Gas Mark 3,*
then *140°–150°C/275°–300°F/Gas Mark 1–2*

Chocolate Chip Cookies

Everyone loves these popular cookies, they are very easy to make, and they taste great.

125 g/4 oz butter or margarine
50 g/2 oz soft brown sugar
1 egg, beaten
150 g/5 oz self-raising flour
125 g/4 oz plain chocolate, finely chopped

grease a baking sheet lightly.

cream the butter or margarine and sugar together until light and fluffy. Beat in the egg, then sift in the flour.

add the chocolate pieces. Mix thoroughly.

put 25 teaspoonfuls of the mixture slightly apart on the baking sheet and bake in a preheated oven, 180°C/350°F/Gas Mark 4, for 15–20 minutes until golden brown.

leave on the baking sheet for 1 minute, then transfer to a wire rack and leave to cool.

Makes 25
Preparation time: *10 minutes*
Cooking time: *15–20 minutes*
Oven temperature: *180°C/350°F/Gas Mark 4*

clipboard: These cookies freeze very well. To freeze, pack them in a rigid container, separating the layers with interleaving sheets of kitchen foil. Seal, label and freeze for up to 6 months. To thaw and serve: leave the cookies to stand in the container at room temperature for 20 minutes. Serve as soon as possible.

Index

A

Anchovies, salade niçoise 194
anglerfish 92
apples
    apple Florentine pie with
        cinnamon and ale 204
    apple pie with almond pastry 230
    spiced coleslaw with curry and
        paprika 186
    Waldorf salad with celery, fresh
        mayonnaise and 182
artichokes
    salade niçoise 194
    stuffed 158
asparagus
    and smoked salmon sauce,
        tagliatelle in 140
    vegetables in cream sauce served
        on a bed of pasta 160
aubergines
    Catalan pork stew with tomatoes
        and 58
    ratatouille 154
    roast vegetable salad 190
    spaghetti in pepper, aubergine
        and olive sauce 142
    vegetable moussaka 156

B

Bacon
    beef Bourguignon 66
    coq au vin 113
    lamb casserole with red wine and
        herbs 53
    minestrone 22
    mussel chowder 26
    pâté de Campagne 40
    penne with mushroom, tomato
        and 139
    savoury soufflé omlette 37
    stuffed artichokes 158
    tagliatelle verde with garlic,
        fennel and 132
    traditional paella 148
    and turnip soup 18

baked
    monkfish with green pepper
        sauce 92
    ricotta cheesecake 226
    scallops with butter and
        breadcrumbs 102
    scones with whipped cream 238
    sea bream with tarragon and
        lemon 86
baking blind 176
barbecued satay lembu 46
basil
    bean soup with 34
Basque-style chicken with garlic,
        ham, tomatoes and
        peppers 114
batavia 180
Bath buns 241
bean soup with basil 34
béchamel sauce 8, 37, 176
beef
    beef Bourguignon 66
    beef Stroganoff 50
    beef tacos 65
    braised, with cheese
        dumplings 48
    fillet steak baked in pastry 70
    pot roast of 44
    roast, with individual Yorkshire
        puddings 62
    satay lembu 46
    stir-fried, with baby corn and red
        peppers 60
    stock 10
beef Stroganoff 50
beurre manié 122
blackberries, fruit compôte with
        summer garden fruits 208
blackcurrants, fruit compôte with
        summer garden fruits 208
bouillabaisse 78
braised beef with cheese
        dumplings 48
bread
    rolls, fresh 236
    wholemeal 234
bread sauce, roast chicken with
        gravy and 106

bream, sea, baked with tarragon
        and lemon 86
brochettes, seafood, marinated in
        fresh lime juice 95
bulgar salad with lemon and oil
        dressing 188
bulgar wheat 18
Burgundy pheasants 120

C

Cabbage, spiced coleslaw
    with curry and paprika 186
cakes
    carrot cake 244
    chocolate gâteau with rum and
        walnuts 246
    rich fruit cake 249
cannelloni
    meat-filled 128
carrots
    carrot cake 244
    spiced coleslaw with curry and
        paprika 186
casseroles
    beef Bourguignon 66
    lamb casserole with red wine and
        herbs 53
    winter vegetable casserole with
        cheese topping 166
Catalan pork stew with tomatoes
        and aubergines 58
celeriac
    winter vegetable casserole with
        cheese topping 166
celery
    stir-fried summer vegetables 164
    Waldorf salad with apples, fresh
        mayonnaise and 182
    winter vegetable casserole with
        cheese topping 166
cheese
    baked ricotta cheesecake 226
    bean soup with basil 34
    cheese dumplings, braised beef
        with 48
    feta, Greek country salad with

black olives and 192
    French onion soup 32
    minestrone 22
    rack of lamb 54
    savoury soufflé omlette 37
    soufflé 38
    spinach lasagne baked with
        cheese sauce 130
    tomato chowder 25
    vegetable moussaka 156
    vegetable pie with potato pastry 176
    vegetables in cream sauce served
        on a bed of pasta 160
    winter vegetable casserole with
        cheese topping 166
cheesecake, ricotta, baked 226
chicken
    Basque-style, with garlic, ham,
        tomatoes and peppers 114
    coq au vin 113
    and olives with fresh herbs and
        garlic 116
    Provençal, with fragrant herbs 118
    in red wine 113
    roast, with bread sauce and
        gravy 106
    savoury soufflé omlette 37
    stock 10
    tequila, in pine-nut sauce 108
    traditional paella 148
chickpea salad with garlic and
        olives 197
chillies 95, 139
    coriander and chilli pesto,
        spaghetti with roasted peppers
        and 145
    fettuccine with chilli, prosciutto
        and tomato sauce 134
    garlic prawns with limes and 96
    salsa cruda (tomato chilli sauce)
        9, 65
    seafood brochettes marinated in
        fresh lime juice 95
    spicy fish stew with peppers,
        limes and 82
chocolate
    chip cookies 250
    gâteau ganache with chocolate

cream filling 224
gâteau with rum and walnuts 246
mousse, iced, with whipped
cream 220
chorizo 148
chowder
mussel 26
tomato 25
cinnamon and ale, apple Florentine
pie with 204
classic fish pie 77
coconut milk 46
coffee
and brandy ice cream 215
meringues 222
coleslaw, spiced, with curry and
paprika 186
cookies, chocolate chip 250
coq au vin 113
coriander
and chilli pesto, spaghetti with
roasted peppers and 145
red snapper with limes and 80
courgettes
ratatouille 154
stir-fried summer vegetables 164
vegetables in cream sauce served
on a bed of pasta 160
crab
bouillabaisse 78
cracked wheat 18
cucumber
gazpacho 30
Greek country salad with black
olives and feta cheese 192
salade niçoise 194

Daurade 86
defrosting 11
desserts
apple Florentine pie with
cinnamon and ale 204
apple pie with almond pastry 230
baked ricotta cheesecake 226
coffee and brandy ice cream 215

coffee meringues 222
fruit compôte with summer
garden fruits 208
gâteau ganache with chocolate
cream filling 224
iced chocolate mousse with
whipped cream 220
raspberry sorbet 218
tipsy cake with sweet wine 228
traditional rice pudding scented
with rosewater 210
treacle pudding with hot treacle
sauce 212
Devonshire splits 242
dressings
French 198
lemon and oil 188
mayonnaise 182, 200
oils and vinegars listed 136-7
spiced 186
vinaigrette 197, 198
duck with oranges 122
dumplings, cheese, braised beef
with 48

Eggs
cheese soufflé 38
coffee and brandy ice cream 215
herb sauce 180
iced chocolate mousse with
whipped cream 220
mayonnaise 182, 200
salade niçoise 194
savoury soufflé omelette 37
traditional rice pudding scented
with rosewater 210
escarole 180

Fennel
tagliatelle verde with bacon,
garlic and 132
fettuccine 140, 160

with chilli, prosciutto and
tomato sauce 134
fillet steak baked in pastry 70
fish and shellfish
baked monkfish with green
pepper sauce 92
baked scallops with butter and
breadcrumbs 102
bouillabaisse 78
classic fish pie 77
fish stock 10
fisherman's soup with a hot
rouille 28
fresh tuna baked with tomatoes,
peppers and garlic 88
garlic prawns with chillies and
limes 96
grey mullet with red wine and
garlic 90
grilled seafood shells with garlic
and mushrooms 98
kedgeree 146
moules marinière 100
mussel chowder 26
prawn gumbo 20
red snapper with limes and
coriander 80
river trout sautéed with almonds 84
salade niçoise 194
savoury soufflé omelette 37
seafood brochettes marinated in
fresh lime juice 95
sole Véronique 74
spicy fish stew with peppers,
limes and chillies 82
steak, kidney and oyster pudding 68
tagliatelle in smoked salmon and
asparagus sauce 140
fisherman's soup with a hot rouille 28
five spice powder 60
flours, specialist 56-7
fragrant rice with vegetables and
cashew nuts 150
French beans
bean soup with basil 34
salade niçoise 194
stir-fried summer vegetables 164
French dressing 198

French onion soup 32
fresh bread rolls 236
fresh mayonnaise 200
fresh tuna baked with tomatoes,
peppers and garlic 88
fruit
exotic 216-17
summer 206-7
fruit cake, rich 249
fruit compôte with summer garden
fruits 208

Game pie 124
garlic
Basque-style chicken with ham,
tomatoes, peppers and 114
chicken and olives with fresh
herbs and 116
chickpea salad with olives and 197
fisherman's soup with a hot
rouille 28
fresh tuna baked with tomatoes,
peppers and 88
garlic prawns with chillies and
limes 96
grey mullet with red wine and 90
grilled seafood shells with
mushrooms and 98
roast vegetable salad 190
tagliatelle verde with bacon,
fennel and 132
gâteau ganache with chocolate
cream filling 224
gazpacho 30
grains 56-7
grapes
skinning 74
sole Véronique 74
Waldorf salad with apples, celery
and fresh mayonnaise 182
gravies, meat 9
Greek country salad with black
olives and feta cheese 192
green salad with a mixed herb
sauce 180

grey mullet with red wine and
garlic 90
grilled seafood shells with garlic
and mushrooms 98
gumbo, prawn 20

Ham

Basque-style chicken with garlic,
tomatoes, peppers and 114
savoury soufflé omlette 37
stuffed artichokes 158
haricot beans
bean soup with basil 34
minestrone 22
herbs 7-8, 184-5
herbs de Provence 118
hygiene 11
ice cream, coffee and brandy 215
iced chocolate mousse with
whipped cream 220

Kedgeree 146

kidney
steak, and oyster pudding 68

Lamb

casserole with red wine and
herbs 53
rack of 54
lasagne, spinach, baked with cheese
sauce 130
lemon, baked sea bream with
tarragon and 86
lettuce
Greek country salad with black
olives and feta cheese 192
green salad with a mixed herb
sauce 180
limes

garlic prawns with chillies and 96
red snapper with coriander and 80
seafood brochettes marinated in
fresh lime juice 95
spicy fish stew with peppers,
chillies and 82

Macaroni 139

mayonnaise 182, 200
meat-filled cannelloni 128
Mediterranean vegetables with
fresh herbs 162
meringues
coffee 222
gâteau ganache with chocolate
cream filling 224
minestrone 22
monkfish, baked, with green
pepper sauce 92
moules marinière 100
moussaka, vegetable 156
mushrooms
beef Bourguignon 66
beef Stroganoff 50
coq au vin 113
fillet steak baked in pastry 70
grilled seafood shells with garlic
and 98
penne with bacon, tomato and 139
mussels
bouillabaisse 78
grilled seafood shells with garlic
and mushrooms 98
moules marinière 100
mussel chowder 26

Nuts

apple pie with almond pastry 230
carrot cake 244
chocolate gâteau with rum and
walnuts 246
coleslaw 186

fragrant rice with vegetables and
cashew nuts 150
river trout sautéed with
almonds 84
Waldorf salad with apples, celery
and fresh mayonnaise 182

Oils, specialist 136-7

okra, prawn gumbo 20
olives
black, Greek country salad with
feta cheese and 192
chicken and, with fresh herbs and
garlic 116
chickpea salad with garlic and 197
Mediterranean vegetables with
fresh herbs 162
spaghetti in pepper, aubergine
and olive sauce 142
omlette, savoury soufflé 37
onion soup, French 32
oranges
duck with 122
turkey and orange stir-fry with
mixed vegetables 110
oyster
steak, kidney and pudding 68

Paella, traditional 148

pancakes, tortillas 65
partridges 124
passion cake 244
pasta
fettuccine with chilli, prosciutto
and tomato sauce 134
meat-filled cannelloni 128
penne with bacon, mushroom
and tomato 139
spaghetti in pepper, aubergine
and olive sauce 142
spaghetti with roasted peppers,
coriander and chilli pesto 145

spinach lasagne baked with
cheese sauce 130
tagliatelle in smoked salmon and
asparagus sauce 140
tagliatelle verde with bacon,
garlic and fennel 132
vegetables in cream sauce served
on a bed of 160
pastry
almond, apple pie with 230
apple Florentine pie with
cinnamon and ale 204
fillet steak baked in 70
game pie 124
potato, vegetable pie with 176
steak, kidney and oyster pudding 68
pâté de Campagne 40
peanut butter, satay sauce 9, 46
Pecorino Romano 134
penne with bacon, mushroom and
tomato 139
peppers
baked monkfish with green
pepper sauce 92
Basque-style chicken with garlic,
ham, tomatoes and 114
fresh tuna baked with tomatoes,
garlic and 88
Greek country salad with black
olives and feta cheese 192
Mediterranean vegetables with
fresh herbs 162
roast vegetable salad 190
roast, in virgin olive oil 175
roasted, spaghetti with coriander
and chilli pesto and 145
rouille (red pepper sauce) 8, 28, 78
salade niçoise 194
spaghetti in pepper, aubergine
and olive sauce 142
spicy fish stew with limes,
chillies and 82
stir-fried beef with baby corn and
red 60
stir-fried summer vegetables 164
winter vegetable casserole with
cheese topping 166
pesto, coriander and chilli 145

pheasant
  Burgundy pheasants 120
  game pie 124
pies
  apple Florentine pie with
    cinnamon and ale 204
  apple pie with almond pastry 230
  classic fish pie 77
  Game pie 124
  vegetable pie with potato pastry 176
pimentoes
  fisherman's soup with a hot
    rouille 28
pine nuts 108
  corriander and chilli pesto 145
  tequila chicken in pine-nut
    sauce 108
pork 11
  pâté de Campagne 40
  stew, Catalan, with tomatoes and
    aubergines 58
  traditional paella 148
pot roast of beef 44
potatoes
  classic fish pie 77
  potato pastry, vegetable pie
    with 176
  rosti 170
  scalloped, flavoured with
    onions 172
  vegetable moussaka 156
prawns
  bouillabaisse 78
  garlic, with chillies and limes 96
  prawn gumbo 20
  seafood brochettes marinated in
    fresh lime juice 95
prosciutto, chilli and tomato sauce,
  fettuccine with 134
Provençal chicken with fragrant
  herbs 118

Quark 244

Rack of lamb 54
raspberries
  fruit compôte with summer
    garden fruits 208
  raspberry sorbet 218
  raspberry vinegar 198
ratatouille 154, 162
red pepper sauce see rouille
red snapper with limes and
  coriander 80
redcurrants, fruit compôte with
  summer garden fruits 208
rice 56-7
  fragrant, with vegetables and
    cashew nuts 150
  kedgeree 146
  pudding, traditional, scented
    with rosewater 210
  traditional paella 148
rich fruit cake 249
ricotta cheesecake, baked 226
river trout sautéed with almonds 84
roast
  beef with individual Yorkshire
    puddings 62
  chicken with bread sauce and
    gravy 106
  peppers in virgin olive oil 175
  vegetable salad 190
rosewater, traditional rice pudding
  scented with 210
rosti potatoes 170
rouille 8, 28
  bouillabaisse 78
  fisherman's soup with a hot 28

Safety, food 11
salads
  bulgar salad with lemon and oil
    dressing 188
  chickpea salad with garlic and
    olives 197
  Greek country salad with black
    olives and feta cheese 192
  green salad with a mixed herb
    sauce 180
  roast vegetable salad 190
  salad leaves 184-5
  salade niçoise 194
  spiced coleslaw with curry and
    paprika 186
  Waldorf salad with apples, celery
    and fresh mayonnaise 182
salmon, smoked, and asparagus
  sauce, tagliatelle in 140
salsa cruda 9, 65
satay lembu 46
satay sauce 9, 46
sauces
  béchamel 8, 37, 176
  bread 106
  herb 180
  rouille (red pepper sauce) 8, 28, 78
  salsa cruda (tomato chilli sauce)
    9, 65
  satay 9, 46
  tomato 8
savoury soufflé omlette 37
scalloped potatoes flavoured with
  onions 172
scallops 82, 102
  baked, with butter and
    breadcrumbs 102
  bouillabaisse 78
  grilled seafood shells with garlic
    and mushrooms 98
  seafood brochettes marinated in
    fresh lime juice 95
scones, baked, with whipped
  cream 238
seafood brochettes marinated in
  fresh lime juice 95
shellfish see fish and shellfish
silverside 44
sole Véronique 74
sorbet, raspberry 218
soufflés 38
  cheese soufflé 38
soups
  bacon and turnip 18
  bean soup with basil 34
  fisherman's soup with a hot
    rouille 28
  French onion 32
  gazpacho 30
  minestrone 22
  mussel chowder 26
  prawn gumbo 20
  tomato chowder 25
spaghetti
  in pepper, aubergine and olive
    sauce 142
  with roasted peppers, coriander
    and chilli pesto 145
spiced coleslaw with curry and
  paprika 186
spicy fish stew with peppers, limes
  and chillies 82
spinach
  lasagne baked with cheese
    sauce 130
  tagliatelle verde 132
starters
  cheese soufflé 38
  pâté de Campagne 40
  savoury soufflé omlette 37
steak, kidney and oyster pudding 68
stews
  bouillabaisse 78
  Catalan pork stew with tomatoes
    and aubergines 58
  spicy fish stew with peppers,
    limes and chillies 82
stir-fried
  beef with baby corn and red
    peppers 60
  summer vegetables 164
  turkey and orange, with mixed
    vegetables 110
stocks 9-11
stuffed artichokes 158
sweetcorn
  baby, stir-fried beef with red
    peppers and 60
  rack of lamb 54
  tomato chowder 25
Szechuan pepper 60

T

Tacos, beef 65
tagliatelle 132, 160
    in smoked salmon and asparagus
        sauce 140
    verde with bacon, garlic and
        fennel 132
tarragon
    baked sea bream with lemon and 86
    vinegar 198
tequila chicken in pine-nut
    sauce 108
thunder and lightning 242
tipsy cake with sweet wine 228
tomatoes
    Basque-style chicken with garlic,
        ham, peppers and 114
    Catalan pork stew with
        aubergines and 58
    fettuccine with chilli, prosciutto
        and tomato sauce 134
    fresh tuna baked with peppers,
        garlic and 88
    gazpacho 30
    Greek country salad with black
        olives and feta cheese 192
    Mediterranean vegetables with
        fresh herbs 162
    penne with bacon, mushroom
        and 139
    ratatouille 154
    roast vegetable salad 190
    salade niçoise 194
    salsa cruda (tomato chilli sauce)
        9, 65
    tomato chowder 25
    tomato sauce 8
    traditional paella 148
    vegetables in cream sauce served
        on a bed of pasta 160
    winter vegetable casserole with
        cheese topping 166
tools and utensils 13-14
topside 44
tortillas 65, 80
traditional paella 148
traditional rice pudding scented
    with rosewater 210
treacle pudding with hot treacle
    sauce 212
trout, river, sautéed with almonds 84
tuna
    fresh, baked with tomatoes,
        peppers and garlic 88
    salade niçoise 194
    seafood brochettes marinated in
        fresh lime juice 95
turkey and orange stir-fry with
    mixed vegetables 110
turnip and bacon soup 18

V

Veal
    meat-filled cannelloni 128
vegetable moussaka 156
vegetable pie with potato pastry 176
vegetable stock 11
vegetables 168-9
vegetables in cream sauce served on
    a bed of pasta 160
vinaigrette dressing 197, 198
vinegars, specialist 137

W

Waldorf salad with apples,
    celery and fresh mayonnaise
    182
walnut-crumb sponge 246
wholemeal bread 234
winter vegetable casserole with
    cheese topping 166

Y

Yorkshire puddings,
individual, roast beef with 62

Acknowledgments

Special photography by William Adams-Lingwood

All other photos:
Octopus Publishing Group Ltd. / Martin Brigdale, Nick Carman, Jean Cazals, Laurie Evans, Graham Kirk, Sandra Lane, Diana Miller, Peter Myers, Roger Stowell, Paul Williams, Trevor Wood.

Home economist
Bridget Sargeson